Catch Me a Poem

by

Monica Toohey Haack

Published by Monica Toohey Haack
540 Belgrade Avenue, North Mankato, MN 56003.
433 Wheeler

Formatted, typeset, edited by Judy Lloyd Anderson, 2031 RoeCrest Dr., North
Mankato, MN. 56003

Clip art from Christian Images – Parsons Technology, Incorporated Software,
Power Up Software, Inc., Corel Corporation, Totem Graphics, Inc., One Mile
Up, Inc.

Cover photograph © 1984 Sr. Noemi Weygant, St. Scholastica Priory, Duluth,
MN 55811. Used by permission.
Photograph page 36 © Ron Anderson, Mankato, MN.

Acknowledgments and Thanks to:

Poet-photographer, Sr. Noemi Weygant, O.S.B. for the cover BUTTERFLY. I send these thanks heavenward for she passed away this summer.

Peggy and Jack Sexton, Holy Spirit Retreat Center, Janesville, MN, for their inspiration, direction and prayers and for permission to use the illustration "Jesus Our Savior" from the cover of Jack's book, *He Himself Will Baptize You in the Holy Spirit and Fire* (Matthew 3:11).

Judy Lloyd Anderson, my generous friend, for her confidence, encouragement and expertise in preparing my manuscript for printing.

For Patricia Johnson (1924-1992), President and Poet Laureate of the League of Minnesota Poets and all my poet friends.

The Craftsman

Words gather in my heart –
a mound of stones.
I free them;
they find their way to my mind,
tumble about noiselessly,
then spill out into my hand.
Eager fingers
guide them
to a creative workshop,
a blank sheet of paper.

A Gemologist
teaches me how to sort,
choose the most valuable nuggets, directs me
as I rub and polish the gems,
shows me how to connect them
with a golden chain,
fashion them into a poem necklace.

This collection is dedicated with gratitude to:

THE GIFT GIVER

I thank you, Lord, for gifts you give
For family, friends, the life I live,
Good health and Nature, gift of pen;
For these I give You praise. Amen.

*Use the talents you possess; for the woods would be very silent,
if no birds sang but the best!*

Also dedicated to:

Mom and Dad,
Louise and Bill Toohey,
who taught us
the Art of Living,
the Joy of Giving.

To My Jim
for his encouragement,
pride in my accomplishments,
his ability to accept my writing clutter,
his understanding when
the "writing bug" bites day or night
and for his help with the household chores
so there is more time for my creating.

My love does not bring presents,
nor sends me flowers or card,
but he shops and he does windows,
chauffeurs and tends our yard.

And to each family member, poet, friend
who has encouraged me, helped me to grow in the art
or just let me know they have enjoyed my writing,

THANKS TO YOU ALL!

Contents

Poetry -- Words With Wings

Seasonal Sampler

Holidays

Love and Family

Looking Back

Faith

Just For Fun

Limericks

Vacation and Leisure

Florida

Arizona

Texas

Friends, Neighbors, School, Community

Foreword

The author of this volume of verse and memories is not a Shakespeare or a Milton. She is a housewife and mother, grandma and friend; she is gracious, loving life and living it to its fullest. She draws from the wellsprings of her heart and mind, sharing her personal feelings and experiences with family and friends. Her own intensity of living, deep religious faith, care and concern for people, break through her writings, which are warmly reminiscent, sometimes sentimental and sparkling with humor and good sense.

Catch Me a Poem is sincerely written and can add a new dimension to the lives of those who sometimes fail to see the beauty in a flowering field or a sunset, who never probe beyond a common sight or do not listen to a voice within.

That this work of love may bring joy to all who read it, is the sincere wish of one who has experienced the devoted loyalty and selfless giving of the author herself.

Sister M. Kathryn

Sister M. Kathryn Mayer

Sister M. Kathryn Mayer, a School Sister of Notre Dame, is now re-tired and living at the Good Counsel Motherhouse in Mankato. She was an English and Journalism teacher at Good Counsel Academy for girls in Mankato, Minnesota, and she served as Associate Editor for "L' Osservatore Romano," English edition of the Vatican newspaper for many years.

A Word from Monica

Dear family and friends,

Finally, here it is – a collection of some of my verses, tributes and memories, gathered from cellar to attic: an accumulation that you might call *expressions of Monica.*

People have asked me when I first began to write poems. It was not during my school years, nor in the first years of married life; about thirty years ago I began composing verses for special occasions and for my own greeting cards.

When Patricia Johnson invited me to join the newly formed Southern Minnesota Poets' Society (SMPS) in 1976, I began to learn more about poetry and to write in earnest. Through SMPS and later membership in the League of Minnesota Poets (LOMP) and the National Federation of State Poetry Societies, I made many wonderful friends and began sharing my poetic efforts in schools, small group meetings, letters and readings on appropriate occasions.

I found that I like to play with words. Some of my poems are light hearted people-poems; others are more crafted forms. I hope you will relate to the lines of my verses. If you happen to pick up this book and do not know the author, please read on, for it will not take long to get acquainted. My themes are not unique – they are about everyday experiences and people. May they touch your emotions — tickle your funny bone, bring a tear or two, tune you in to God or spark a memory. Enjoy!

Monica Toohey Haack

Monica Toohey Haack

Welcome to My Kitchen

This is my favorite spot in the the home Jim and I have enjoyed and treasured for thirty-nine years. In our kitchen I have prepared meals (somewhere over 40,000) of good solid food and goodies. I love to cook.

Family and friends have gathered around our table, shared food, light and laughing banter, serious discussions, and fellowship. Here also I create my crafts, write letters, poetry and pray. It is my precious "place".

I believe that when we create, we are truly alive. Whether constructing a concrete building or cementing a relationship– at work, at home, at play–smile! Create an air of happiness around you.

So, bake a batch of cookies, challenge a computer, soothe hurts, sing a song. Long ago Benjamin Franklin penned these wise words, *"Waste not time, for time is the stuff life is made of."*

Poetry -- Words With Wings

My words and feelings,
cocooned within an affectionate heart
and excited spirit, emerge
a butterfly
that wings its way
into many lives.

Come Fly With Me

The Gift of a Poem

Catch me a poem, a bright butterfly;
grasp gentle words as they flutter by.

Find me a poem in dewdrops and rain,
in snowflake, in windsong, in frost on the pane.

Whisper a poem, a light lyric of breeze
murmuring softly in midsummer trees.

Paint me a poem, portraying a thought
colored on canvas, a memory caught.

Sculpt me a poem in marble – not clay–
of long lasting words that will not wear away.

Build me a poem, a bridge framed of steel
connecting the thoughts that you and I feel.

Delight me with verse – rhyming or free –
a sonnet, an ode, villanelle, elegy.

Uplift my spirit in love song or prayer;
dream me a poem and I walk upon air!

Real Communication

We hear each other speak;
words are tossed, caught,
but to really communicate,
both the ears and heart
must learn to listen
and then —
        there is silence.

I Write Lite

I sift old thoughts that I have kept
and seek new themes; seems I'm adept
at making just the commonplace
perk up your ears, light up your face.
I touch you with some words, oh yes,
they're not profound, but nonetheless
the words I write are warm, sincere,
the kind of words you like to hear.

My poems are filled with laughter, tears,
with sunshine, love, with rousing cheers.
I write to comfort you; it's plain
you ache inside, I share your pain.
My volumes won't be bound in gold,
I won't be famous when I'm old,
nor will I shake the world apart,
my goal is just to LIGHT your heart.

To my poetry friend, Toi Rochovitz

Burnt Offering

I checked the clock, time was fleeting,
hustle, bustle, had a meeting.
Began to cook a batch of rice,
then curled my hair, so I'd look nice...
made my bed and swept the floor,
heard a horn, rushed out the door.

The meeting done, my friend returned
me home to find the rice all burned.
"Yes, haste makes waste," I've heard them say;
I found it sad, but true today.
I should have set the burner dimmer
and kept my thermostat on simmer.

No Wonder

My grandpa, Hugh Toohey, was postmaster in the old home town, Fulda, Minnesota. My dad, Bill, was his assistant. My husband, Jim, was both clerk and carrier for the Mankato Post Office for 27 years. Perhaps this is why my life has been A LETTER with a Love Stamp attached.

You Betcha

For price of a stamp
you can send the gift of YOU;
still the best bargain in town.

Choice MaleMan

He goes his rounds, this trusty gent;
bad weather ne'er delays him.
Jim is my fav'rite mailman, 'cuz
he brings no bills, just pays 'em.

A Letter

A letter:

L ove offering with tidbits of news tucked inside an
E nvelope. Bubbling over with personal happenings,
T opics of mutual interest, questions, answers, feelings, it
T ouches lives, bonds spirits.
E ach writer and receiver shares a gift of time and hearts'
R esponse.

When I Write You a Letter, I Hug You With My Pen

When you're not here beside me
and your presence is denied me,
in a letter I will hide me
and I'll hug you with my pen.

When not close enough to hear me
nor nearby so you can cheer me,
in a letter you'll be near me
and I'll hug you with my pen.

You see the words I write reveal me;
in my letters comes the "real me."
When you read them, hope you'll feel me
hugging you with my pen.

Time Wise

I could try to write a sonnet
But, I find my time spent better
When I forget to be a poet
And just pen a love-ly letter.

Writing letters is a passion for me. Letters coming and going are an important connection that makes my life special, exciting, and filled with love. In addition to my personal letter writing, I have served as Corresponding Secretary for the Southern Minnesota Poets' Society (SMPS) for fourteen years, for the League of Minnesota Poets (LOMP) for seven years, and was personal correspondent for Holy Rosary Catholic Church for ten years. I have enjoyed every minute of this pleasurable, rewarding hobby-commitment.

Monica

A blossoming poet is Monica.
Unlike Moore, she plays no harmonica,
But she lightens our hours
With sunshine and flowers
Bright daisies and pansies, japonica.

She says she's not in the same bracket
As those in the poetry racket,
But at writing a letter
Nobody's better,
There Monica really can "Haack" it.
                                        Norman R. Boe

Thanks to Norman R. Boe, poet, mentor and great friend, who recognized my letter writing talent along with my poetic beginnings. Norman, a long- time member, past president, membership chairman and Poet Laureate Emeritus of the League of Minnesota Poets, died in October, 1995. He will be sadly missed.

On Wings of a Poem

My well of poetry is dry –
"Where are the words?" I muse and sigh.
My eyes look up, birds skim the sky,
then, inspiration fills my well;
ideas excite, delight, compel.

Poem of birds becomes my goal
an ornithologist my role.
I bird-watch and I pigeon-hole
the words and birds, then take my pen
with fancy free-- to write again.

A robust robin heralds spring,
invites a cardinal to sing,
proud bluejay flaunts a white-tipped wing.
My heart ascends, like air-borne birds;
a poem takes flight on bright winged words.

The Lost Words

My pen lies idle
while noiseless winds of anticipation
toss ideas about
in my head, in my heart.
I am alone with my thoughts.
Where are the words?

Busy-ness Syndrome

Words that gnaw and grind and grate,
words that I have learned to hate,
words I'd like to give the gate –
"I'M TOO BUSY NOW."

Words that banish time for fun,
words, excuse, "I've gotta run,"
words, a promise? "When I'm done.
I'M TOO BUSY, NOW."

Words that hurt and bother me,
words in answer to my plea,
words I'd banish, Yessiree!
"I'M TOO BUSY NOW."

Words belie the acts of care,
words that say, "No time to spare,"
words might mean sometime we'll share,
"I'M TOO BUSY NOW."

Words I do not wish to hear,
words are not for me, my dear,
words might bring a tiny tear,
"I'M TOO BUSY NOW."

Other words I promise you,
words, I hope you'll give me too,
words our spirits will renew,
"I'M BUSY, BUT I'LL FIND TIME FOR YOU."

Seasonal Sampler

Seasoned Minnesota

Seasons, smorgasbord of weather,
reasons I remain at Minnesota's table.

Pleasing me with original recipes a Master Chef creates,
teasing me with tantalizing sights, tastes, aromas.

Savoring fresh crisp greens of spring, I dine,
flavoring life with piquant dressings.

June tosses sweet berries into my bowl of summer,
soon I give in to a second helping.

Fall, I heap my dish with veggies buttered with sunshine,
call on family, friends to join in thanks-giving.

Bold winter offers frozen sweets, snow pudding;
cold, we are warmed by coffee served by a cozy fire.

Gratefully, I relish Minnesota cuisine.
Platefully speaking, its menu is a unique, served with flair
Buffet Bonanza.

House Call

March closes the door of winter,
creaking with winds that sting,
turns the knob that opens my door
to the delights of spring.

Fresh April, washed by raindrops,
tiptoes my steps today,
rings the doorbell, leaving for me
a basket full of May.

May-time empties out her basket
brimful of gifts too soon,
then departs to give her place
to warm and playful June.

Bright springtime leaves reluctantly
as summer comes to call;
I hoard each season's pleasures,
but I love spring's most of all.

Thanks to Elvira T. Johnson for reading this poem at SMPS' first hosting of the LOMP seminar in Mankato. She is Poet Laureate Emeritus of the League, an inspirational poet, critic and friend.

Shower Gift

Scattered crystal beads
glisten in amber-glow lamplight,
become onyx gems –
raindrops on blacktop.

Eyes Spy

Eyes spy Spring's First Prize,
a dainty violet nods
and whispers, "Pick me! Pick me!"

Welcoming Committee

Nature's alarm rings,
wakes hibernating spirits,
bids them to greet Spring.
Trees wave "Hi" with green-gloved hands,
sunray fingers touch with warmth.

Raindrops splash "Hello!"
Furrowed earth grabs eager seeds,
breeze tips jaunty kites,
birds and children sing her song.
Spring takes a bow and scampers on.

No Vacancy

A pair of small birds
found their dream house,
but it was already
"wrented."

Rescued

Dainty violets
cower among blades of grass
awaiting their doom.

Executioner,
ready for the beheading,
hones mower's dull blades.

Fair lady dashes
to rescue the small blossoms;
long grass bids farewell.

Violets now pressed,
framed. Grass mown, blown;
new spears soon regrown.

May-baskets (or My, How I Have Changed)

Fond memories of yesterday
flood my heart and seem to say
May-basket Day is here and so
my mind turns back to long ago
when Mother's busy hands would make
baskets, goody-filled, to take
to friends, and oh, it was such fun!
I'd ring their bell and then I'd run.

But that was in a time long past,
now I wouldn't (couldn't) run so fast.
Like Mom's, my baskets are quite bright,
crepe paper flowers ruffled right.
I'll hang my basket on your door
and since older, I like kissin' more,
I'll ring the bell and then I'll wait;
I have permission from my mate
to stay and claim the prizes missed
when I ran too fast to be caught and kissed.

Re-leaf

Raindrops and sunshine
    explode budding trees
        into green canopies;
new leaves add color to
    earth-paintings of
        spring and summer.
Earth-gifts push through the soil –
    I contemplate the miracle
        of Springtime.
A catchy TV commercial asks
    "How do you spell relief?"
        I spell it SPRING!

Pansy Gifts

Plant-presents grow in rich black sod,
buds open, blossom-- hand of God.
Small perky faces 'mid the flowers
are brushed by breeze, refreshed by showers.

Bright pansies smile as if to say,
"Hello, enjoy this sun-drenched day,
but let us be to bloom awhile."
I nod, and then return each smile.

Some other pansies look at me,
"Please pick," it seems their silent plea.
I gather some, fill crystal vase
to lend my kitchen simple grace.

The extra ones I dry and press
these garden-gifts my hands caress.
Now I will share their charm with you,
still lovely as when touched with dew.

June-Night Bedtime

I lay down my sleepy head,
my pillowcase
has caught the freshness
of a brisk breeze in its folds
and I smell summer.

Treasure Trove

When Summer comes, I welcome her;
she holds me with her powers.
I see her beauty glow and grow,
she splashes in her showers.

I watch as sun-soaked children play
build castles in the sand.
I view the Artist's color splashed
on canvas made of land.

The wrens wing by and dot the sky,
gardens offer pleasures.
I thank a great Creator for
His wealth of golden treasures.

When Summer fades she leaves behind
bright joys to stash and hold,
to keep my spirit warm and snug
when winter winds blow cold.

Lake Superior Treasures

A handsome, gray haired gentleman
and I are having lunch
at a Lake Superior picnic overlook.
We reminisce about trips and vacations
on this same route —
our honeymoon,
tenting with 1 - 2 - 3 - 4 lively lads.

I close my eyes, see once more
large boats, choppy waves, Duluth Harbor;
we watch the Aerial Bridge open, close,
visit Split Rock Lighthouse,
Gooseberry Falls.

We camp out near Kakabeka Falls,
Ontario, Canada,
watch the foaming tannish brown water
tumbling over the rocks.
I hear a boyish voice explain,
"Oh, look, Mom, Dad, it's Root Beer Falls."
I open my eyes; there are just the
two of us.

I clutch yesterdays to my heart
thank God for this, Our Today.
A chipmunk sneaks up, steals a
fallen cracker.
No-one, nothing, can rob us
of our North Shore Memories.

The Sun Connection

Water skis skim lake,
cut ribbon rays of sunlight,
leave path of foam, waves.
Ripples calmed, golden threads mesh,
fill life with mended sunbeams.

Air Show

Autumn-tinted leaves
        drop
from summer-spent trees.
Miniature colored parachutes
swirl
    twirl
drift
        land--
    ground covered with Fall.

Catch As Catch Can

brief time
leaf time
colored blaze
grasp these
clasp these
splendored days

beamy
creamy
harvest moon
cold winds
bold winds
all too soon

Winter's Bride

Summer leaves our midst today.
This gracious lady goes her way,
throws us a kiss.

Now silver-touched, once golden hair,
like frost-fringed breath of Autumn air,
flows gently with the wind.

Her leaf-print gown with burnished sheen,
a mix of colors, fading green,
blows with muted harmony.

Bold Wintertime admires Fall's charms,
catches her in strong, cold arms,
knows he needs her warmth.

He courts with diamonds and with lace
'til Springtime comes with charm and grace,
shows him she also cares.

Her cheeks afire with rosy-blush,
Spring melts his heart, his icy rush,
glows, accepts his proposal,
confidently whispers, "I do."

The Last Word

A shiny new chimney
puffs smoke signals --
scrawled on the sky,
an elm tree epitaph.

A Taste of Winter

Outside my window
our crystal village glitters–
chicken soup bubbles.

Beyond my window
wind-tossed feather flakes snow pile–
warm "iced" sweet rolls tease.

Winter Acrostic

Winds that whistle, whip and blow,
Icicled roofs and drifting snow,
Naked branches quiver, shiver,
Thin ice, thick ice on the river,
Endless hours spent shoveling—
Remember, they do lead to Spring.

Winter Green

Jim putts white golf balls
on living room carpet-green–
'til Spring comes, of course.

Beauty Treatment

Sky powders Earth's nose
then lightly dusts her ashen cheeks
with soft white snowflakes.

Bank Statement

March deposits blizzards and flurries
into huge drifts and snow banks;
welcome, warming sun melts the accumulation.
Wind withdraws loose dirt and soil,
blows it about,
drops it atop remaining frozen assets.
Cleansing rains wash away each vestige of winter,
    closes out its account.

April opens a new Spring Account.
Funds of perennial and newly-planted seeds
are released; we watch them grow.
Sky entrusts a wealth of priceless raindrops.
We re-invest our savings
    of excitement and appreciation.

The Banker computerizes, checks,
sends out statements,
calls attention to Spring assets.
We watch the account balance increase
    with compounded interest.

Holidays

New Year's Eve Table Blessing

Bless us, oh Lord—
    who are Your friends.
    As we share this meal,
    the old year ends
    and we greet a New Year
      together
      WITH FAITH.

And these Thy gifts—
    upon our table; grant us good health
    and thus enable
    us to meet each new day
      WITH HOPE.

Which we are about to receive—
    to accept and believe.
    You have given us gifts,
    touched them
      WITH LOVE.

From Your bounty—
    from Your heart;
    as we share Your gifts,
    our voices ring out
    in prayer
    for a peace-filled
      HAPPY NEW YEAR!

Through Christ our Lord—
    Amen,

      WITH GRATITUDE.

Be my Valentine

Valentines don't have to be
hearts and flowers and lace,
with a cupid shooting arrows,
cunning smile upon the face.

It is sharing an expression
any day, of light, bright cheer,
of thoughtfulness, concern and love
for someone far or near.

It may be a card or letter
or a short call on the phone,
a little visit now and then
to a someone who's alone.

It is extending joy and laughter,
a handshake, hug or tears,
a friendly favor, compliment,
or calming someone's fears.

We give, receive these valentines
and never even know it.
This is a chosen, extra day
to care much and to show it.

On this paper one I'm sending
are the simple words I CARE.
You know it, but it seems my heart
must show, must tell, must share

the feelings I can't seem to hide
when close or far apart.
I offer you, my Valentine,
a crooked, homemade heart.

Kissin' the Stone

When you visit o'er in Ireland,
Blarney Castle can't be missed
where eloquence is promised,
but the stone must first be kissed.

You lean out a high-up-window,
upside down and hanging prone,
someone grasps your legs, holds on tight,
lips brush the Blarney Stone.

Will words now be more eloquent?
No matter true or phony,
when one lays on the blarney,
it's labeled "pure baloney."

Flag Day

Flags flapping, whipping, or quietly draped proclaim
Love of Country, Liberty. This red, white and blue bunting is our
   declaration of patriotism. We honor
America, our Land of plenty, beauty, opportunity; we promise to
   enjoy, defend, take care of it—our God-given gift. We salute Old
Glory and with gratefulness we support our nation.

Duty-bound, yet freely, we pledge our
Allegiance to the Flag of the United States of America, our
Yardstick of DEMOCRACY.

Mother's Day 1970

Thank You, Mom

Thanks, dear Mama, for your loving
arms, around me through the years,
for the times you shared my laughter,
helped to wipe away my tears.

Thanks for all the re-made dresses,
grudgingly worn, hand-me-down.
Really, truly, they were nicer
than those on the rack uptown.

Thanks for smoothing out the wrinkles
in my winter underwear,
for sharing prayers and caring thoughts,
finger-curling stubborn hair.

Thanks for birthday cakes and parties,
for May-baskets, "Gifts of You,"
for the many times you went without
when you bought me something new.

You and Dad taught us that family,
whether near or far apart,
is a precious gift to cherish
and to hold close in the heart.

Mother's Day 1992

It is over twenty years now
since you left us, yet you're near,
and because you left sweet memories
we still feel your presence here.

Easter Punnies

The Easter Bunny had a beer
      before he made his stops,
      filled to the brim with Easter cheer,
      was also full of hops.

I left a fat, crisp carrot out
      hid, watched the rabbit grabbit.
      The Bunny left my basket, then
      she hid and watched me nabbit.

The farmer fed his chickens mash
      shaded yellows, greens, pinks, blues,
      kept hen house hot, his hens laid eggs
      hard boiled of many hues.

The Bunny's mind, preoccupied
      with health and aging legs,
      dropped Easter basket, realized
      he hadn't cooked the eggs.

Afterglow

I watch excited children
scamper up and down our street;
they ring our bell, hold up their sacks
and call out "Trick or Treat."
Parents bring their little goblins,
ghosts dressed in sheets of white,
midst the older witches and monsters
who are on the prowl tonight.

My lighted jack-o-lantern,
with his warm and toothy smile,
sits welcoming my callers.
In between I muse awhile...
the Halloweens of yesterday,
the hub-bub and the noise
when costumed "trick-or-treaters"
included our four boys.

I drop the goodies into bags,
my reverie is broken;
I deeply feel the joy of NOW
as I hear a child's words spoken.
A familiar voice just bubbling over
says, "Grandma, don'tcha know
it's me," then grandson John unmasks
and my heart takes on a glow.

It is quiet now, the lights are out,
my Halloween complete.
Each trickster who had come tonight
brought ME the special treat!

Strictly Spooking

Hallowed eve
Arrives on the brink of November.
Little goblins bob with delight,
Lighted jack-o-lanterns grin.
October revelers call "Trick or Treat,"
Witches whoosh on broomsticks,
Excitement reigns supreme,
Eerie costumed creatures cavort.
Nothing pleases and teases like

HALLOWEEN.

Thanksgiving Fate

Mr. Tom turkey meets the ax;
the gobbler is undressed,
redressed;
the gobbler gets gobbled.

November Brings

cold winds
bold winds
snow falls
snow balls

icy street
cold feet
snow boots
warm suits

and Thanksgiving day!

Christmas Presence

A Christmas tree grows in my heart,
its roots reach deep, each branch a part
of happy times I've lived, and now
fond memories cling to every bough.

Though growing still, its branches hold
bright lighted candles, tinsel, gold,
warm friendships that I share each day,
a star on top to show the way.

I add new ornaments each year,
memories, treasures, people-cheer.
Some packages are wrapped and tied
with bows and lots of love inside.

Yet, what makes Christmas real for me?
A manger scene, with Christ Child--see
The One who shared NATIVITY--
HE IS THE GIFT BENEATH MY TREE!

Christmas Connection

CHRISTMAS TIME and I conjure
MAIL that makes my spirit dart,
CREATES a chain, of this, I'm sure,
A gift to treasure in the heart--
NECKLACE of love, both strong and pure
OF cherished feelings, looped and linked--
GOLD friendships shared, that will endure.

Christmas Was Made for Grandmas

I can see the spirit of Christmas
in baby Brian on my lap.
In his night cap and red sleeper,
a tiny Santa takes his nap.

I can hear the Christmas Spirit
as John "ohs and ahs" with glee,
though he didn't find his two front teeth
in a package 'neath the tree.

I embrace the Christmas Spirit
while hugging Jennie, two years old,
our own little Christmas angel
with hair of shiny, coppery, gold.

I am touched by the Christmas Spirit,
feel the infant Christ Child near.
I see Jesus' smile reflected
in each face that I hold dear.

I will hold this special feeling
as this Christmas I remember,
for its glow is everlasting—
it has warmed a cold December. (1978)

Color Me Red
(Red-Faced, that is)

My Danny begs, "Oh, Mama, please
come to our Christmas play."
Since Peter is a wiggly two,
whatever can I say?

I think awhile and then decide
if Peter starts to roam,
or giggle, wriggle, make a fuss
then I'll just take him home.

We get there late, the seats are filled
and so, alas, alack,
late-comers, we are forced to stand
along the wall in back.

Then fourth grade class begins to sing.
I hold Peter up to see,
and Danny spies us standing here–
he waves to Pete and me.

I am so proud of little son;
he has behaved so well,
when suddenly his hand shoots up
and rings the fire bell.

There's lots of bedlam for a while,
then teacher calls out, "Whoa!
No need to leave; there is no fire.
Let's get on with the show."

I took my little culprit, scrammed,
my face a Christmas red.
Next year you'll note our absence;
we're staying home instead.

The Lasting Gift

A round jolly man with beard white as snow,
Sits talking to kids, I hear his "Ho! Ho!"
He's dressed in red suit with white furry trim,
Excitedly, children draw close to him.

A curly-haired girl climbs up on his knee,
Right then I remember old Santy and me.
Completely enchanted and safe in his arms,
I share in his laughter, Santa Claus charms.

"I hope you've been good," I hear Santa say,
"What gift can I bring you on Christmas Day?"
"Oh, just a few clothes and a trinket or two,
I don't want too much, I'll leave it to you?

And when I get down, he spies my small tear,
"Santa, can't Christmas last all through the year?"
With eyes a-twinkle, a smile on his face,
Santa spoke these words that time can't erase--

"Remember this well that love is the key
that opens the door to life's mystery.
When Christmas giving is over and past,
Loving assures us THE SEASON will last."

Star of Hope, Star of Peace

Rosemary hangs the star
above the cherished Christmas stable,
the one her Bill so lovingly crafted
for their first holiday, forty years ago.
Treasured figurines, though faded and chipped,
glisten as brightly
as Yesterday's memories.

Bill's will be a heaven-spent Christmas,
yet she feels his presence as
her stereo softly plays "O Come All Ye Faithful."
She can still hear Bill's ever familiar
resonant voice.

She sings along,
brushes away a tear,
begins to mix the dough
for her Christmas cut-outs.
Grandson Ryan, a serviceman overseas,
will be waiting for a Care-Box
of Grandma's cookies.
He can only dream of a white Christmas.

Reindeer, trees, and bells are cut,
baked, layered with good wishes.
On top she places a star-shaped treat
sparkling with sugar and love –
a symbol of hope, a symbol of peace.

Lovingly, she sends Ryan
a taste of HOME.

After Christmas Conundrum

Santa brought a salad shooter.
I guess he didn't know it,
instructions throw me for a loop--
each time I try, I blow it.

The plastic cones have metal parts.
They're slicers, mincers, graters,
for fruits and slaws and vegetables
cukes, carrots and potaters.

And so I take it from the box,
the challenge of the ages.
I study diagrams and then
assemble it in stages.

It seems I put a part in wrong.
This really makes me dizzy,
the thing's supposed to save me time--
instead, I am more busy.

The veggies fly and then they land
in the bowl or on the floor.
I must've read directions wrong--
so I try and try some more.

Next year, old Santy, will you bring
a present I can handle?
I think I might, could light the match--
if you would bring a candle.

Love and Family

Love Can Be

a wide and flowing river
a gurgling, glistening brook
a treasured, pleasured memory
a pressed flower in a book

a newly planted garden
a field of ripened grain
a quiet breeze, a rushing wind
a cloudburst, gentle rain

the promises of springtime
the summer sun's warm blaze
the burnished leaves of autumn
the winter's waiting days

the words of honest sharing
the heart that freely sings
the feelings joined together
the true love God gives wings

Love Song

Wind:

Air in motion,
any stream of air,
air blown to force or produce
a musical sound.

It begins with a light puff of interest,
continues with a breeze of caring,
blows with a steady burst of understanding,
swirls with a current of thoughtfulness,
creates music in our souls.

We listen with our hearts,
thank God that
we have been caught up
in its frequent gusts of affection.
Love is the best of winds.

For Jim:

One Yellow Rose

I remember dear, the time, the place
a single rose in crystal vase,
your kind blue eyes, your precious face.

This day you pledged your love to me
I dried rose petals, potpourri,
the fragrance sealed in memory.

Marriage Vows

See our golden bands
bright promise
that we shall meet Life
travel its highway
hand in hand

Marriage Premium

with open eyes and wide awake hearts
watching cherished dreams come true
holding precious memories
a devoted couple sees children, grandchildren mature
learn how to hang on, how to let go
we share a common bond
with a heritage of togetherness, support
we treasure family ties
watching cherished dreams come true
with open eyes and wide awake hearts

(Marriage Premium can also be read from last line to first line.)

Boat Trip

(Jim and Monie ages 33 and 26)
In '52 we went to sea
my brand new hubby, Jim and me.
We sailed on waters deep and blue,
though sometimes waves
would spoil our view.

Young sailors, we had much to learn—
how to chart a course,
know stem from stern.
But we worked so hard to steer our boat,
that now we're just content to float.
(Jim and Monie, ages 75 and 68)

Best Buy

In 1951 my wardrobe consisted mostly of green and white striped cotton "Princess Peggy" frocks from Salet's basement which I wore to work at my foiks' Ice Cream Store. When the LaVogue Dress Shop advertised its big annual Half-Price Sale, I decided it was time to buy myself something classy and I headed downtown.

I spied, tried and "buyed" a bright red suit, blowing a whole month's salary— forty dollars! Although I scooped a lot of ice cream to pay for that suit, it turned out to be a fantabulous INVESTMENT.

One Sunday morning, dressed in my new outfit, I attended Mass at Holy Rosary Church in North Mankato . I happened to sit in front of a good-looking bachelor, Jim Haack. Evidently, my red suit caught his eye and he recognized me as a grade-school classmate of his youngest sister, Leona. He called to ask me for a date. I thought if Jim was as likable as Leona, I should accept. I guess we both knew right from the start that this was IT. We dated for a year and our love grew. We were married at St. John's Church in Mankato on June 24, 1952.

James and Monica Haack, June 24, 1952

Twenty years later, a colored photo of me wearing that suit and a little story I had penned for our boys about how it had sparked our romance, prompted the manager of the LaVogue shop, Patricia Johnson, to invite me to join the newly formed Southern Minnesota Poets' Society. Wisely, I accepted and so, once again, my red-suit purchase changed my life.

I think I must say it was forty bucks well spent.

For Jim, my dance partner of 43 years

So, Who Needs Arthur Murray

My date and I dance at the Kato Ballroom in July of 1951.
I whisper, "This is a waltz, and we're not waltzing."
Jim blushes, "I really don't know how."
My turn to blush, "That's okay,
we'll just glide around in time to the music."

Can you believe, he dated me again,
asked me to be his life's partner?
Marriage changed our two-step into a one-step.
Four baby boys taught us the Colic Walk–
one-two-three-waah,
and the Two A.M. Bounce–
bottle-burp-hug-step-hug-pat-pat-burp.

We polkaed, one-two-three-hopped, after pre-schoolers,
bunny-hopped grade-schoolers to school, parties, games,
rocked through the tumultuous teens with high-schoolers.
Boys grow up, move out onto Life's ballroom floor.

My retired date and I sit at our kitchen table;
the radio plays our song,
"The Green, Green Grass of Home."
"Let's dance."
We move ever so gracefully across our ballroom floor.
We still haven't learned the fancy steps,
but we do agree, it's a really great DANCE.
How well we glide with the music!

We began a tradition of a wedding wishing well which holds this thank you poem. The wishing well was originally a marshmallow barrel from the Toohey's Ice Cream Store– later used as a toy box, finally for weddings, beginning with nephew Gregg and Bonnie Bibbs' wedding.

Our Wishing Well

A Wishing Well is for Wishes.
So on our Wedding Day,
we're grateful for your wishes.
In return we'd like to say,

"Drink from our cup of Happiness
of Hope and Love and Cheer.
God keep and bless each one of you
that both of us hold dear."

You've come to help us celebrate
with wishes warm and true;
we hope the bubbling joy we feel
bubbles over onto you.

With friends and family 'round us,
we'll start our married life.
What could be a happier beginning
for a husband and a wife?

The wedding cake, the card, the gifts,
the music, laughter, flowers,
the lovely gowns, "well-suited" guys,
pictures, memories — OURS!

We've said our vows, exchanged our rings
we're filled-to-the-brim with caring.
"Thank you so much for bringing YOU!
Wedding Days are for sharing."

What God has united, man must not divide.

Lord, today we exchange our marriage vows, begin our life together, create a new family. We ask Holy Spirit to guide us that we may retain our own personalities, yet have our lives blend into the oneness of our marriage.

We thank you, dear God, and our parents for the precious Gift of Life that you have given us. We are grateful to our mothers and fathers for their constant care and support, for their friendship, values and ideals which they have instilled in us. We want all of our family members and friends to know that we are thankful for them also, for without them, life could not be as bright and wonderful.

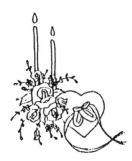

This is our marriage prayer to Jesus, who performed His first miracle at the Wedding Feast of Cana.

Please bless our marriage, show us how to live and grow together. Send us the gift of children, give us the grace, strength and patience to rear them with the same love and concern that we received from our parents. Keep your caring arms around us, always help us to be kind and understanding to each other, faithful to our commitment. Remind us often that happiness cannot be bought nor is it found in material things alone. Instead, it is found in the generous sharing of self.

This is the Miracle of God's Love,
This is the Miracle of our Love for Each Other.

For our children, their children and theirs.

The Inheritance

You are the songs that we sing
the poems we have begun.
You are the sun, moon and stars
that brighten our days,
light up our nights.

You are the flame on our candle of love,
the smile on our lips, the tears in our eyes.
You are the answers to the prayers we have prayed,
the dreams we have dreamed.

Life is an adventure, a game, a gift –
pursue it, play it, cherish it.
Sing along with us,
write your own special songs and poems,
dream new dreams, make them come true.

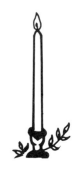

Listen to, talk to God in prayer,
share laughter and tears.
Be a light to family and friends.
Keep us ever in you hearts,
share generously and with joy
OUR LEGACY OF LOVE.

David, Peter, Mark, Danny Haack, 1965

Dave & Mary Haack & family

Dan & Joanna Haack

Mark & Kristen, Brian, Matthew Haack

Pete & Kelly Haack

*To our dear families scattered far and wide, no matter how distantly
we are related, I, a bit selfishly, claim you as mine.*

Relatively Speaking

If I can say to you
And you can say to me
"You are related and my friend"
we are both twice blessed.

41

Special Credit

Mother:

I lie unnoticed beneath your heart;
an unseen Hand commences a journal
of my unborn life,
daily records my growth, my feelings.

It has been twenty-one days
since my life began,
I feel my heartbeat;
I feel yours too, pounding anxiously
as you struggle with your problem
of an unplanned pregnancy.
You are frightened, not ready for me.

Please do not let the pages of my journal
be torn from you,
thrown in the waste heap. I want to live, grow,
love and be loved.

Four months have passed,
I feel your calmness now;
you heard my embryonic plea,
made your decision.
I am a miniature adult,
all organs and systems are present.

I have been growing for six months,
nourished by the food you eat,
lulled by the rhythm of your heartbeat;
I am warm and secure.

Nine months have gone by;
it is time for my birth.
I am a real live baby;
I thank God and you for this gift of life.

Yours or other caring hands take over,
record my new beginnings,
fill my needs, give me love,
register my growth.

God smiles. He whispers to me
assuring me that I am His child,
that I shall always be
a very special entry
in His Journal of Life.

Hope For Tomorrow

Children light our lives with sunshine
Hope and dreams create and share,
Into our hearts they bring their gladness
Love so deep, beyond compare.
Daily add their warmth and sparkle,
Rest assured they help us grow,
Every child, unique and precious,
Needs God's love and ours to glow.

Presents of Joy

We of God's family
are gifts for each other,
packaged with love,
given and received
with gratitude—
cherished.

The Story of the Eternal Daisy

Julie Sexton, the sixteen year old daughter of our friends, Jack and Peggy Sexton, was killed in an automobile accident. At the time of her death, Peggy asked me if I would write a poem for Julie. I could not find the right words at that time, so I made a dried flower picture memorial from blossoms in her bouquets. When I lamented to my sister, Charlotte, that some of the daisies I had chosen had some petals missing, she remarked without hesitation, "Monie, that is where you will find a poem."

Later that summer we attended the wedding of Lisa and Les Fleury (Charlotte and Roy's daughter) in San Jose, California. On the flight home, I reflected on the happy time we had shared together as a family. Then, my thoughts turned to the recent sorrow of our friends. (Friends are family too.) I felt a poem in the making, took pen and notepad from my purse and the words flowed. When I got home, I gave the poem to the Sextons and it did bring them comfort. As time went by, I continued to share the Eternal Daisy poem with others as well. Now, sixteen years later, I have seen my poem move and touch lives far beyond anything I could have imagined.

I am thankful to Peggy for suggesting that I write a poem, and to Charlotte for her faith in my words and for sensing when there is a poem deep within me waiting to break free.

I am also grateful to Pam Lamm of North Mankato for her lovely illustration and calligraphy that has made my poem even more meaningful.

The Eternal Daisy

God fashions the family
    as He creates the daisy–
        growing profusely
            in all kinds of soil;
                its roots hold fast.

Sturdy leaves form
    on graceful stems
        that bend gently
            with the wind.

A bud bursts into bloom.
    A family of dependent petals
        support each other
            and cling to the golden center
            of God's love.

With a bright floral face
    turned heavenward,
        each daisy matures individually–
        part of a vast field.
            Side by side they grow and touch.

As each petal falls,
    God tenderly takes it in His hand
        to reassemble,
        until one day
            His blossom is complete.

The Family is God's Eternal Daisy.

The House We've Lived In

Our house, on the corner of Belgrade and Sherman in North Mankato for thirty-eight years, has big bright rooms filled with love, treasured heirlooms, wall-hung photographs, homemade poems, clutter and collectibles. Jim claims I save EVERYTHING. Being on the approach to both Veteran's Memorial and North Star Bridges, we can literally sit on our front porch and watch the rest of the world go by.

A very special feature of our location is the Belgrade United Methodist Church across the street. Its friendly members adopted me years ago and I began my poetry readings at their Ladies' meetings. At night the lighted cross lends a feeling of faith, peace, and security.

Here we happily, hecticly raised four fine sons and now we reside more quietly in the Senior Lane. The Welcome Mat is always out for we both enjoy visitors. Honestly, we are never too busy!

If "Home is where you hang your heart," this is where we have hung ours.

Little Boys Rhyme

The question is, "Just what are boys?"
They're lots of energy and noise–
with cars and trucks and baseball bats,
guns and holsters, cowboy hats.

Trikes and bikes and roller skates,
stockings with evasive mates;
they bait a hook with wiggly worm
and snicker, watching Mother squirm.

Boards and hammers, can of nails,
good desk drawer may house their snails;
puzzles, books and games galore,
dirty clothes behind the door.

They keep you jumping, on your toes
with chicken pox and runny nose.
They're very dear, I'll tell you this,
I hoard my pay– each jam-smeared kiss.

Framed Memory

My kitchen window is a frame
for a picture dear to me,
our boys out playing baseball
climbing Moses' apple tree.

I open up the window, call,
"Come get a treat, you boys."
It's strange,
they hear these words so well,
but not, "Pick up your toys."

Oh, why is it they seem to run
as fast as they are able
except when I need help and yell,
"Come in and set the table."

Though they keep me in a tizzy,
they're sweet as they can be.
I thank our dear Lord every day
for sending us these three.
[Dave, Mark and Danny
and seven years later, Peter]

For Pete

Sideline Mother

I go to every football game,
you see, I'm Pete Haack's mother.
But to tell the truth, I do not know
one goal post from the other.

The players scamper here and there
as though they're in a muddle,
then stop and make a circle, which
Pete's father calls a huddle.

But oh, I watch for Number 9
and try to keep my smile up
while fans yell "Haack" and down he goes
far underneath a pile-up.

And next I cheer to beat the band,
for now my Pete is scoring.
My mother pride wells up inside
while Scarlet fans are roaring.

At season's end, Pete's football done,
I'm to the world reporting,
the game seems dumb, but this I know,
I'll miss my son's cavorting.

Mom Wants a Basket!

Pete's a fine basketball player;
he gives the game all that he's got,
gets up before daylight to practice;
this sport and his team mean a lot.

He aims, then shoots for the basket
and sometimes the ball sinks right in;
not discouraged, though, when he misses,
he keeps trying and trying again.

Such zeal, such determination,
he could use taking care of his clothes.
He consistently misses the basket
when his socks and gym shorts he throws.

Do you think this could be a solution,
hang a hoop on the back of his door?
With a hamper beneath and a board to record,
would Pete keep on trying to score?

For Dave, Mark and Danny

Three Teens at a Time

I look back now to teen-aged years
of long-haired boys and tuned-out ears,
of motorcycles, clunker cars,
loud music played by weird rock stars.

Back then, the by-word was "Rebel,"
at times I was compelled to yell.
I wondered if we'd make it through
these crucial times, your Mom and you.

You kept me guessing, boys, you know,
but, yes, we helped each other grow.
I walked the floor, you stayed out late,
in spite of it, you turned out GREAT!

Shoe Revue

I look at the pair of tiny, tatted booties
lovingly Grandmother-made,
framed on my bedroom wall.
They set in motion, a heart-parade
of boys' shoes.
White soft-soles, outgrown, bronzed,
brown hi-tops carry toddlers' feet,
tattered tennies track mud across
the kitchen floor of memory.
Boots and skates frolic,
growing athletic shoes
move with dexterity on a field or court.
Rented patent leathers dance by;
jobs, college, marriages, careers
pull grown-up shoes in new and different directions.

The pace changes,
the present generation of boys' shoes
is joined by little-girl slippers.
I am filled with the music of
Yesterday's parade;
it swells with the addition and excitement
of today's new beat.
I remember it all began
with tiny tatted booties, forever
heart-framed.

Play Ball

The day is hot, the bleachers filled;
it's a crucial game today.
The pitcher's pitch, the batters bat,
while the fielders field the play.

One team will win, the other lose;
but both teams and fans, the same,
know that all good sports are winners;
they lend spirit to the game.

Mother's Day 1995

The year my oldest son was married, I sent a letter to the Editor of the Mankato Free Press, Ken Berg rejoicing over having a girl in the family. Calling it a "reverse-twist to the customary Mother's Day tribute," he used it in his column. Now I have four lovely daughters-in-law; each of them is very special to me. I dedicate this column to each of them.

For Mary, Kristen, Joanna, and Kelly, gifts presented to their Mom from four fine sons.

I have celebrated Mother's Day-- as a daughter, grand-daughter, sister, niece, wife, daughter-in-law, mother of sons, and now as a mother-in-law.

There have been times (never having had a brother) when I wondered if I could survive this motherhood bit in a male-dominated household. My dreams of a daughter to cook with, to do things with, to share with, gave way to the reality of a rough and tumble, take apart, on-the-run, paper route, ball playing, telephone and doorbell ringing, loud music, bicycle, motorcycle, clunker-of-a-car world, and all the other forms of chaos a family of all boys seems to create.

Now suddenly my boys are growing up. My one son has married and presented me with an ally in a very special "almost daughter."

I'd like to say this to her: I know we will have a very happy relationship because already you have shown your thoughtfulness in numerous ways. You have brought out many wonderful qualities in our son that I knew were there, but had not surfaced. The two of you complement each other so nicely.

I am proud of the way you do things together. Your way of life will reflect both of your families, but most of all it will be a blending of ways that will be your very own life-style.

It is with a chuckle that I sit back and listen to my son explain where you can get the best pot-roast for the money, or how nice it is to do things together or "my wife says..."

You are an accomplished wife and homemaker. Isn't it strange that your cookies (the same recipe as mine) taste so much better? How's that for a switch on the old cliche, "just like mother used to make?" I'll gladly take a back seat to you, for now my son's happiness is in your hands.

For each of you who claim my fellows for your own, I want you to know this: your happiness, your feelings, your wishes are just as important to me as my sons'. I know they aren't perfect, for they possess many human frailties -- lots of them inherited from a very human ever-lovin' Ma.

I do hope, though, that we have instilled in them a sense of responsibility to others and to themselves.

To Re-feather the Nest

Alone once more we share our quest
with new identity we seek:
feathery tufts for empty nest.

We find more time for friends, fun, rest
while spirits flicker, often weak:
alone once more we share our quest.

Such quiet thunders, we attest
while searching, sight a bit oblique:
feathery tufts for empty nest.

When young, we grew as life progressed
now still we grow, yet not antique:
alone once more we share our quest.

We realize that we are blessed.
Love and cherished memories speak:
feathery tufts for empty nest.

Grown children state, "You folks are best."
Their children – grand, fun, joy, unique:
alone once more we share our quest
feathery tufts for empty nest.

For Jim: The Game

Retirement had just begun,
I found out golf was great, what fun.

I've putted, chipped in rain and sun,
I've shot for par of course (no pun).

Enjoyed the greens when GAME is done,
I'll feel I've scored Life's "hole in one".

Grandparenting

For our precious grandchildren and greats: John, Jennie, Brian, Matthew and ? and John's children Tyler, Brianna and ?

When grandchildren begin to make their appearance,
a parent's life takes on a totally new dimension.
We re-learn how to change diapers (with disposables)
mix formula,
"kid kuddle,"
get reacquainted with the rocking chair
(no matter how we've tried to avoid it).
We put our work at hand on hold to spend quality time with them,
to get to know each other well.

We play lots of old, long-forgotten games, and new ones too,
go to ball games,
discipline (well, sort of)
read stories,
cut and color,
watch cartoons on TV,
sing, laugh, dry some tears.

It's quite a challenge to keep up with them.

A Grandma has to be sure her cookie jar is never empty.
A Grandpa has to have a ready fishing pole,
a baseball mitt,
keep boards, hammer and nails ever ready.

We watch them grow, but all too soon
these grandchildren are all grown up-up-and-away,
have children of their own.
Then, finally,
we really are GREAT
and not just PLAIN.

My grandson John once remarked that I was his PLAIN grandma and Jim's mother was the GREAT grandma.

For Grandson John Haack

Skates for Sail

John skates on by with boyish ease,
like sailboat caught in summer breeze.

He sails on ice with such delight,
his hockey skates dart left and right –
swift sails that move him out of sight.

My memories are crystal clear,
Jim, I, our boys, all skated here.
I brush away a Grandma-tear.

The wind of youth is brisk and strong,
puffs me and skaters right along,
while speakers blare a skating song.

I feel the sting of winter's blast,
but I am warmed as John glides past.

Oops, John is down upon his knees;
he's up, sails on, with boyish ease.

For my red-haired beauty, grand-daughter, Jennifer Lee Haack

Tutti Fruitti Cutie

Jennie, you're the apple of my eye,
spicy and sweet as the applesauce
simmering on the back burner of my Magic Chef.
I'm plum crazy about you, you know.
Your burnished strawberry tresses
accent your soft creamy skin,
your cherry lips speak quietly.
A girlish giggle escapes now and then,
your mouth wears a cherished grin.

You are tall and willowy
as a young and supple "Haack"berry tree.
Colorful and healthy,
you add a zesty flavor to my life.
You a-peel to me
like a ripened-just -right banana;
your personality bubbles like lymon Sprite.
You're as warm as a just-out-of-the-oven
blueberry muffin, a delight
to my Grandma heart's appetite,
with eyes that sparkle like clear grape wine,
a peach in my Basket of Life.

I love to have you come and share
your fruit-filled life with me.
Sometimes I wait for you, but patiently,
like waiting for a fresh pineapple to ripen.
The waiting is worth it, you come.
We have a tasty visit. I'm thankful
we're so closely related, "orange" you?
I think we're a pretty good pear, Jennie,
You will always be the apple of my eye,
A REAL TUTTI FRUITTI BEAUTY.

Brian's Unexpected Guests

His mother gave a party,
when Brian James turned three.
He had invited lots of guests,
including Gramps and me.

His friends from Storyland all came
and so did all his toys.
Most of the neighbor kids were there,
the house rang with happy noise.

Of course, his mommy made a cake,
lit candles numbered three.
He huffed and puffed and blew them out,
clapped chubby hands with glee.

He opened up his presents, then
his birthday cards galore.
He spied another gift he'd missed,
with wrappings on the floor.

He opened it and added these
to the gifts he'd gathered:
C.B., red car, Boss Hogg's white hat;
seems he'd asked the *Dukes of Hazard*.

For Grandma Jean, now in Heaven, who loved to tell this story.

Fish Story 1980

Brian, aged five, fishing from the pier at his other grandparents' lake home, kept pulling in small perch as fast as he could cast out his line. He couldn't believe his good luck until Aunt Paula exclaimed, "Brian, you've discovered a school of fish."

Brian was delighted with the number of his catch, but evidently not with their size; for the next day, as he marched off with his pole, he announced, "Today, I'm going to get the Teacher!"

For grandson Matthew Haack – July, 1989

Matthew is 3, Going on 4

Our little grandson, Matthew three
years old; is filled with energy,
has precious own identity.
He talks to playmates we can't see,
with charming geniality,
such unsophisticated glee,
his laughter, "whys," delighting me.

A treasure for our family,
he stands by Mom. Still he is free
to roam about, use liberty
with mischief, spunk, timidity.
He smiles a lot; with big tears, he
can melt one's heart. (How can one be
upset?) With "Open Sesame"
to Adventureland, he needs no key.

He romps with playmates noisily
or plays alone quite quietly.
His days are filled, I guarantee,
with people, fun, variety.
We hug him to us joyously.
He hugs us back, but boyishly,
loves Brian, Dad, with equity,
his company's a pleasantry.

We thank our dear Lord ardently
for this small child – so trustingly
an open book, yet mystery,
our little grandson, Matthew, three,
Going on four.

In memory of our nephews: Gregg Bibbs
(1946-1976) and Jeffrey Bibbs (1952-1992)

The Clock

Your Great-grandma Prigge's clock
on the shelf in your parents' bedroom,
ticks off the minutes, hours,
chimes memories of you, dear Gregg.
I remember a four-year-old's hands
taking this clock apart
in "Mema" and Grandpa Toohey's bedroom,
curious to know what made it run.

Seventeen years later,
your twenty-one-year old jeweler-helper's hands
reassembled this treasured time piece.

The hands on the clock of your life
stopped suddenly, Gregg;
a divine Clockmaker rewound its mainspring,
and with loving hands,
placed it on the shelf of eternity.

We synchronize our heart's clock with yours;
they tick with the togetherness of family.

Still Shining

With eternal sunshine, Jeff
wears an everlasting smile.
Thoughts of him stir warm and happy memories,
bring tears, tug at my heartstrings.
Ever a wonderful son, husband, father,
family member, friend.
I will feel my dear precious nephew,
hugging me for always.

For Irene Toohey, a loving teacher-Aunt

Achievement Test

Aunt Veronica lifts the notebook
from the trunk, hands it to me.
I open it, it holds a teacher's notes,
notes belonging to a special aunt —
Aunt Irene's school journal.
Fifteen years ago she said her last good-byes
to loving family, friends, students.

I read the notes:
Bicycle Program, Gym – April 6;
Failing slips after 4 weeks;
Achievement Tests – April 20-24...

The familiar script fades;
an instant photo emerges.
I see her smiling Irish eyes;
her hand gently clasps mine.

Today I will play the teacher,
add a final note to yours;
October 18, 1979
Achievement Test – Irene Toohey–
HEAD OF THE CLASS.

For Uncle George Toohey

The Godfather

Like a sturdy dependable railroad tie,
he helps to hold up the steel on the track
that we travel,
a train of family.

In Memory of Mark Callahan September, 1978, son of my cousin Janet and husband Bill Callahan.

Promise

Mark's spirit lingers,
sparkling as the silver ripples
of Lake Keesus.

I see it growing,
just as this small spruce tree
planted in his memory
grows here in Callahan's yard.

It is as sturdy as the sentinel pine
that guards his grave
in the little country cemetery.
It reaches across an ocean,
memorialized in a tree planted in
Israel by friends of his family.

Mark's Mom and I
sit in the September sunshine,
we do not speak.
I know we are both feeling
his presence.

Colored leaves drop,
remind us that Summer is gone,
Fall is upon us, soon to be followed by Winter.
But just as the seasons pass,
the Winter of Death is followed
by the budding, greening, flowering
of an Eternal Springtime.

This is God's promise.
I take Jan's hand,
together, we hold onto this Hope.

Monica Martha Toohey, age 5

Looking Back

When I was a little girl, just so high

(a line from a verse I recited long ago)

I arrived on the scene in Fulda, Minnesota on May 19, 1926. My first home was a small ancient house, originally the first school house in Fulda, located on the bank of Second Lake, just outside the "city" limits. My parents had a dairy farm and milk route.

My older sister Bernadette and I would help Dad deliver milk before school in the morning and after supper at night. I wasn't a "dyed in the wool" farm girl. In fact, I was really a "scaredy cat." I did herd the cows, but I kept my distance, believe me. I'd pry the hens off the nest with a stick to grab their eggs and run. It must have been another reason why Dad and Mom moved off the farm to Mankato to start an ice-cream store.

The house where I was born.

Dad's Poem

(*Same beat as Song of Hiawatha, with thanks to Longfellow.*)

Enjoyment was a game of baseball;
played life's game, same joy and fervor.
Met and married Louise Prigge,
dairy farmed and worked together.
Blest they were with precious daughters,
taught that family is for sharing.
Handsome, wholesome, manly, gentle,
warm and loving, our dear Daddy.
Poor health forced them to a moving
to Mankato, Minnesota.

Ice cream Store a new beginning;
people came for goodies, friendship.
Dad made ice cream, Mom ran business,
we girls worked with dedication.
Place for kids to meet and mingle,
spot for dates and fam'ly treating.
Cookie cones and nickel malteds,
sundaes, sodas, juke box music.
Sometimes fun, but lots of hours,
Store for us became our whole life.

Childhood Revisited

Three sisters romped in the pasture,
dodged mini-mounds of peat,
gathered marsh marigolds,
skipped smooth stones in the creek,
    went wading in the lake.

People traveling the rural road
saw three small girls –
artists dabbling their lively colors
on a country canvas,
    painting picture memories.

Today, we leave grown footprints on this road;
the pasture, now a county park, is alive;
carefree picnickers
beckon us to share "their" spot –
    but, WE discovered it!

Lake entices; we wade in,
splash water on each other;
summer sun and nostalgia warm our homecoming;
we float on ripples
    of remembering.

Edwin & Bernadette Bibbs, Jim & Monica Haack, Roy & Charlotte Mullin

Sister Act

Bernadette

Yours is a calm and bright spirit
that everyone admires.
You are always there, for family
and friends alike, never too busy
to be a someone to count on—
one who cares, listens, helps.
With treasures of handwork, sewing,
and your special kind of
"Bernie's Love"
You gift us, not just with words,
but with a ready hand and heart.

Monica

Bernadette, first born, Mom and Dad's
pride and joy.
Charlotte, cute, cuddly, curly-haired
baby sister.
Me – warmed in the middle.

Charlotte

You create and share
your neat and warm, love-filled home.
You weave your pattern of thoughtfulness into friendships;
you sing your songs
of faith and life
with sentiment.
Your caring is your craft,
your creation.
God has blessed you,
for you see and experience Him
in His people.

Banana Split

When my life is at its best,
I look back to the days
when I worked
at Dad and Mom's Ice Cream Store.
I say,
"This is really like
Toohey's Specialty of the House, a
BANANA SPLIT!"

The crystal dish of my life
holds sweet and fruitful treats for me.
Each day is like a firm banana
divided, heaped high
with three scoops of home-made
ice cream
the chocolate, vanilla, strawberry
of my delights—
people, faith and meaningful work.

The variety of flavors is enhanced
by rich, sweet, tasty toppings:
the smooth chocolate sauce of thoughtfulness,
fresh berries of generosity,
pineapple chunks of caring,
both yours and mine.

This creation is covered
with the whipped cream of happiness,
sprinkled with the nutty crunch of laughter,
then topped with the cheery cherry of content.

"I have an extra spoon...
Will you share this concoction with me?"

For Grandpa, Peter Prigge, August 28, 1885-December 24, 1932

Christmas Mourning

Grandpa
takes a final breath.
Grandma comforts us,
closes the shoe shop door; parlor is
readied.

I am six,
learn of death,
of family togetherness, love;
sleep in heavenly peace, dear
Grandpa.

Tree moved,
presents put away.
Grandpa in his casket,
pink flowering cactus
bouquet.

Christmas
morning finds us sharing
hurting hearts, memories, tears;
we feel Grandpa's
presence.

For the Grandmas: "Mema" (Louise Toohey) and Bernie Bibbs

Grandma's Magic Fingers

She stitches these with loving care:
    cowboy shirts, flouncy skirts.
Her handiwork seen here and there:
    stylish clothes, buttons, bows.
Simplicity or patterned bold–
    faces glow, grandkids know
the magic Grandma's fingers hold.

The Debut, A Golden Memory

You may not know it, but I am a star in my own right.

St. Gabriel's School of Fulda, Minnesota,
introduces you to the feminine lead,
Monica Toohey
of its grade school Christmas operetta
The Toyshop
December 22, 1935

My Mom-made, ruffled, white crepe-paper costume,
her gold beaded treasure
sparkling on its bodice,
transforms me from a mere mortal
into an inhabitant of Fairyland.

Bright Eyes, the Christmas fairy,
pirouettes around the stage,
waves her wand,
sings her lines.

My excitement was overwhelming.
Now I must confess:
I mixed up the stanzas
and sang them in reverse.

The male lead, my pal Wally,
"Tackhammer the Toymaker,"
still lives in the old hometown.
Whenever we meet, we reminisce about
the olden days of readin' and 'ritin' and 'rithmetic
and always about our stage debut together.

The golden curls have turned to gray;
I'd have just a little trouble pirouetting.
But for a moment,
turn back the clock, and picture me
A Star.

Dreams Fulfilled

Yesterday, when I was young

A pillow slip
hugs brunette pin-curled locks,
a satin case caresses my cheek.
I drift off into dreamland;
I am a queen.
My robe flows about me,
royal gold; it somehow looks and feels
like its matching sheet,
smooth and elegant to the touch.

Today, and not so young anymore

My white permanented curls
rest on a dainty, rosied pillow case.
I lie on sheets of cotton polyester.
My royal night-dress
is a soft, rose-splashed granny gown.

Cozy and sleepy,
I say my prayers,
count my blessings.
No need for dreams of regal stature
for this happy wife, Mom, Grandma, friend,
I AM A QUEEN!

Preferred Identity

If I could have a choice, you see
and someone asked, "Who would you Be?"
I'd answer quickly, "Naturally,
there is no doubt, I'd still be ME."

SCRABBLE ANYONE

My favorite Scrabble partner, Mother,
invites me to play the game.
We build words on a game board
divided into small squares,
with wooden-lettered-and-numbered tiles,
then vie for highest score.
It is an experience of friendly competition,
silence, laughter, entertainment, learning.
Scores are doubled or tripled,
depending on the placement of the tiles
on blue and pink colored squares.

Life challenges me
to play its game on a giant Scrabble board.
This game has different rules:
there are both partners and opponents
with no specific turns.
Each day we clear away yesterday's tiles,
begin a new encounter. We build new words
with involvement, difficulties, risks and caring.
Scoring depends on our actions,
their position determined by the colored squares
of timing and circumstance.

The total score is unimportant;
the emphasis is on –
HOW WELL WE PLAY THE GAME!

Serenity

We search for calm,
find a quiet place
of joy
and love
in embracing arms
of family.

Patchwork Treasures

I snuggle beneath Mother's treasured patchwork quilt;
when sleep evades me,
I mentally begin to connect
my own bright quilt blocks of memories,
    fashion my own poetic comforter.

When Springtime comes, I fold Mom's heirloom gift,
store it until snow flies again.
In the Winter of my life
I curl comfortably
underneath my piece-worked coverlet,
    keeping my spirit toasty warm.

I recount pleasured recollections
    and sleep with peaceful gratitude.

A Matter of Taste

I remember Mama's kitchen.
Yes, I recall it very well,
the Home Comfort range that gave us
the taste of toast and apple jell.

Mama toasted homemade biscuits.
My mouth watered and the smell
would tantalize 'til my tongue touched
the taste of toast and apple jell.

But that was in the long ago.
Now electric toasters work so swell,
like magic, boys transform sliced bread
to taste of toast and apple jell.

Four lads have shared our bread, our life
bring joy to where we dwell,
have popped Life's toaster satisfied,
like taste of toast and apple jell.

Forever Friends

I had a dream the other night.
I heard Grandma's cupboard speak.
I wondered who was listening,
then I heard her rocker squeak.
It seems they were remembering—
oh, what stories they did tell
of happy times and sad times,
children's secrets guarded well.

They recalled the home and garden,
apple trees and flowers in bloom,
while Grandma hustled, bustled 'bout
in her kitchen living room.
The two spoke about my Grandpa,
sitting in his cobbler's chair,
as he soled and heeled the old shoes,
making new ones with such care.

Yes, they talked about their friendships,
Love that lasted through the years,
this rocking chair and cupboard
who shared laughter, memories, tears.
These two antiques kept chattering,
then I woke up with a start.
It only was a passing dream,
but their visit touched my heart.

The Pick Up

A little dresser, time-worn, quaint,
with drawers that stick and peeling paint,
I want to cry.

We set it on the curb, surprise!
It disappears before our eyes.
I say good-bye
to childhood memories.

Mother's Ring

Mother is gone, keepsakes divided;
Grandma's oak table becomes my treasure.
One day it will belong to one of my sons,
I polish it with pride.

My dusting hand wears Mom's mothers' ring,
three small, individually set birthstones–
pearl, emerald, diamond–
clustered in a wide gold band.

I stop dusting, finger the ring,
remember Mom's creative hands.
She is here.
She speaks softly, pulls me close,
a Polaroid heart-print catches her smile.

Mother, you are forever.
Daughters, we are birth-gems
joined together in sisterhood and friendship,
set deep, held fast within the circle of your love.

Mom's Flower Garden

Mother had a way with flowers
She'd talk to them and weed for hours,
survey them with a gardener's pride,
then cut bouquets to take inside
to fill her vases with fresh blooms,
their sweet perfume to scent her rooms.
I wait each year for Spring to come
and then remember Mom's green thumb.
I wonder just what words she chose
to coax the peonies and rose.

For my dad, Bill Toohey (1894–1966) and mom, Louise (1897-1973)

Gilt-Edged Securities

My heart is a strong, safe bank;
cherished in its vaults I keep
Certificates of Friendship;
some are old, some new, filed deep.

There is one for every true friend
who can see another's need,
who reaches out with love, concern;
each one, gilt-edged, indeed.

Every day they grow in value;
they are wealth I cannot measure.
My Heart-Bank keeps them safe for me,
these friendships that I treasure.

My parents, William and Louise Toohey, examples of friendship.

Golden Anniversary Celebration

John and Mary Haack, September 23, 1966

"Grandpa, tell us a story
about the good old days,
how you met and married Grandma,
when you fell for her winning ways.
When you married Grandma,
did you have a car?
Did you take her dancing?
Did you wish upon a star?

"Well kids, this is how it was:
I worked on the Swenson's farm.
Mary was Anna Swenson's sister.
Boy, she sure could cook, had charm.
I had no car to court in,
just a buggy and a horse.
We danced and wished upon a star.
All couples did, of course.

I asked her Dad, Jake Molitor
for his daughter Mary's hand.
Now fifty years have come and gone
since she took my golden band.
Just as the marriage vows proclaim
"It's for better or for worse."
Many times the bills piled up
with no money in the purse.

But it seems we always made it;
God would always see us through.
Our children and our grandkids
helped make our dreams come true.
With hearts that overflow with love,
a smile and brushed away tear,
we both thank God for all His gifts
and for this our golden year.

For Jim's Mom at Mankato House, May 1988

Mother's Day Promise

Though house is quiet, empty now,
its rooms are filled with memories.
Here family shared laughter, tears
and grew in love throughout the years.

The house is sold. "We'll keep the keys
of Home in heart"– our solemn vow,
though house is quiet, empty now.

From My Garden

March 16, 1990

I stand behind the lectern at Holy Rosary Parish,
look down at the white draped casket
of Mary Haack, Jim's devoted Mom,
hold back the tears that gently water
the feelings in my heart.

I begin to read my family poem, The Eternal Daisy
in memory of her and Jim's wonderful Dad, John.
I will always remember them in their garden,
seeding, weeding, hoeing, eagerly picking flowers,
harvesting peas, beans, beets, and plump red tomatoes,
now they enjoy an Eternal Harvest.

Today, I share my kind of flowers,
words seeded, grown, heart-held;
I pick the freshest, brightest stems
for my memorial bouquet
and offer them with love.

For Jim, 1989

Family Album

I page old photo book and see
you – brother, only son.
I watch you grow, see you at play,
seem part of it, your yesterday.
I live your joy of family,
important days, great fun.

Between its covers tucked inside
are memories I weave:
you in knickers, cap and gown,
convertible with top rolled down,
uniformed with Air Force pride,
in service, home on leave.

This treasured album, ours to share
since I became your wife.
We've added pages of our own,
a Mom and Dad, four sons now grown.
Old pictures glued, secured with care,
new faces light our life.

Growing Older and Wiser

dear we've let down our defenses
each learned to listen share as friend
our hearts now link more easily
for we have truly learned to bend

Faith

The Invitation

God invites us
        to come
                follow Him,
to serve
        with faith.
He promises us
        heavenly gifts.

A Child's Letter to God

on Thanksgiving Day

Deer God our techur said we shud rite you a lettur so here goes I hop it dont make you cry cuz I dont like to see peepl ball thank you for my bike, dog, my folks and turkey I I better not forgit my sistur or Ill get crowned hapy thanks Day to you gudby your kid Mikey I hop teachur gives me a gud mark.

The Colors of Hope

With a brush of Love
God arches
a rainbow of Hope
on a easeled blue sky

*About the same time I began to write poetry, I found another hobby –
drying, pressing, and framing flowers. The gifts go hand in hand.*

A Real Posie Picture

You are a blossom
bright with the color of God's love,
a flower, hand picked, enjoyed.
Pressed, preserved, framed
in my heart, you will be
cherished always.

Bountiful Harvest

My
garden
of love grows.
Caring words, deeds
make it fruitful; I tend it,
weed out my faults, then reap its
bounty.

Alpha Betical
Christian Danke Shoen

Artwork
Blossoms
Children
Daylight,

Earthgifts
Friendships
Gladness
Home bright,

Ice cream
Jesus
Kindness
Love-willed,

Music
Nature
Oneness
Peace-filled,

Quiet
Raindrops
Sunshine
Trees, shade,

Unique
Verses
Words shared
X-rayed,

You, Lord
Zealous, gifting to me
   ever blessing
A, B, C, D.

*For Sisters Roberta and Kathleen
Rother and Sisters Honora and
Flavia Elsen (real-life sisters) on
their 50th jubilee and for all
SSND's*

SCHOOL SISTERS OF
NOTRE DAME

Sisters
Caring
Honest
Obedient
Organized
Loving

Sincere
Industrious
Sharing
Trusting
Energetic
Responsible
Selfless

Orderly
Family-minded

Nuns
Our Lady
Thoughtful
Religious
Enthusiastic

Dedicated
Artistic
Motivated
Ever God's chosen ones.

The Gentle Critic

Life is a volume of poetry,
each God-created person
a contributing poet.
We write verses
with the pens of our lives;
some are smooth, lyrical,
others lack rhythm,
are off-beat.

The Editor of Life
lays out a pattern, shows us
how to create the perfect poem,
yet He accepts our finite submissions
with patient understanding.

I am confident that
when I submit my Life's poem
it will be judged
with fairness and love.
When I lay down my pen,
I pray that the Divine Critic
will welcome me with these words,
"Well done, good and
faithful poet."

Lord, Let It Always Be Spring In My Heart

An icicle of resentment
hangs from the roof of my heart.
I try to break it off, chip it away,
but it is frostbound
until the warm sunshine of your forgiveness
melts it away.

Ecumenically Speaking

Understanding fellow Christians with
No denominational barriers to keep us from sharing Faith, we
  each belong to our own chosen church family.
Individually, we may choose traditional vocal and private prayers
  and meditation along with Bible readings to help us grow spiritu-
ally.
Together, touched by the Holy Spirit, we join in praise, petition
  and thanksgiving, discover the oneness in serving
Yahweh, our God.

The Master Craftsman

God fashions His love
into a necklace of gold,
a silver bracelet for each of us.
Each durable, delicate link connects,
forms a continuous chain of caring,
that fastens with a sturdy clasp of understanding.

God gifts us with these precious presents
to be cherished and appreciated.
They enhance our appearance,
enforce our feelings of security
in that love.

He challenges us
to create our own golden, sterling chains
of concern, compassion, involvement
to wear and give
to others.

RENEWAL

Renewal calls, God leads the way,
   we hear His Word to serve and pray.
Each risk we take, each task we share
   in Jesus' name becomes a prayer.
Nourished with love and Spirit-filled
   we follow Him as He has willed.
Every gift He gives becomes a prize
   to use for Him, to evangelize.
World's people cry in pain and strife,
   He breathes through us, new hope, new life.
Almighty God tells us we must
   give praise and thanks, adore and trust,
Lift burdens, share, whene'er we can
   and live in peace with fellow man.

River of Life

This ecumenical faith gathering
brims with praise of
The Father
music jubilant, soft, reverent
gift of tongues, prayers of
please and thanks, listening,
caring friendships shared, strengthened;
Jesus is
present in each worshipper as
love overflows with
The Holy Spirit.

Tempest Tamed

Tyrant tornado, you conceive your plan
to cause destruction.
You blow with harsh breath,
change gentle air angels to swirling devils.
Anger –
a tornado, wild winds funnel, touch down,
destroy the spirit.
Storm clouds may gather,
but God calms troubled winds,
tempers hearts with peace.

Still Here

Why
did they abandon
this House of God?
What force pulls me here?
Piano, exposed strings,
stands bereft in its corner
remembers its yesterdays.

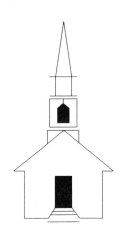

I can feel God's Spirit
as wind whirls leaves.
Memories of worshipers
are caught in decaying rafters.
I hear a long ago choir sing,
a hymn being played
on silent strings.

The Divine Cobbler

He fashions sandals for us
from Life's leather,
to follow His footsteps
on the path Homeward.

Imperfection

I know You understand us, Lord,
Maker of mortals.
Please accept our imperfections.
Each day spark us anew:
Revitalize our spirits,
Feel our deep and vital Love, keep our
Eternal rewards safeguarded.
Calm our troubled, restless spirits,
Teach us how to make choices.
Instead of hanging onto guilt, help us to
Overlook our imperfections with trust in Your forgiveness
Now and forever.   Amen.

Portrait of Friendship

I dip my brush into a hodgepodge of colorations
on the Palette of Life
to create one of my original friendship paintings.

I splatter an array of primary colors
and blended hues on a waiting page:
pinks, reds of affection and love,
indigo, the largess of loyalty,
vibrant greens of growth,
bright yellows of joy,
oranges of honesty,
soft blue shades of togetherness.

Earth-toned brush strokes of practicality
mingle with fuchsias of fun,
purples of patience,
blacks of sorrow,
softened by whites of compassion.

I splash on gold, silver and coppery accents
of communication, availability and understanding.
My unpatterned caring creation is framed
with the weathered wood of acceptance.

Raindrops

The Lord
      hosts a people shower for me.
He sends me family and friends
      like drops of
         His falling
            rain.
I receive them with delight;
they make me bud, grow, bloom.
I soak up this outpouring;
      the overflow of happiness
         splashes off on others,
      gathers in pools around me.
Mirrored in the crystal surface,
      I see the face of
         The Rainmaker.
My gifts are wrapped
      in the sunshine of
         God's love,
tied with His ribbon of rainbow.
I respond with an open heart
      and gratitude beyond measure for
His
      shower
         presents!

Give Thanks

A small, small phrase – no, very big,
there is no doubt about it.
We must put this charge to work
just whisper it or shout it;

"I thank you" is the phrase I mean,
each one of us must tout it,
appreciate and say it now,
for life is less without it.

Crayon Master

God made His world a color book,
its pages filled with hills, sky, brook.

He laid out colors he would use,
chose from the gentle pastel hues
light pinks, soft greens and shaded blues.

Sometimes His artwork is quite bold
with red, orange, purple, yellow, gold—
His masterpieces we behold.

This Artist shows what contrast means.
He blends earth tones with vibrant greens,
crayons black on night time scenes.

Today I woke, to my delight
the earth had been crayolaed white.

I praise God's wonders when I look
and see the beauty of His Book.

Sacrament of the Anointing

We bring our illness, pain, nerves taut,
our lives with worries, trouble-fraught
with hurting hearts, deep-rooted fears,
sad eyes that hold back unshed tears.

The priest anoints with holy oil
foreheads and hands that touch and toil.
We beg our gentle Lord to heal;
we feel His touch, His presence – real.

He gives us hope and strength each day,
time for work, for prayer and play.
He offers love that will not cease;
He heals with Sacrament of Peace.

This Donkey's Destiny

This donkey has no need for speed,
nor dreams to be a prancing steed.
He keeps his steady, plodding pace,
no urge to dash nor win a race.
He treks towards his destiny.

No wish for fanfare, saddle bright,
he is content to share this night
with Joseph, Mary – full of grace –
resting in this lowly place.
He knows his destiny.

He stands in awe with ox and sheep
while angels sing the Babe to sleep.
This donkey claims his honored space.
His eyes behold the Christ child's face.
He thus fulfills his destiny.

Another Donkey's Destiny

This donkey waits for Master's call
here in this cramped and musty stall.
He wonders, will this be The Day
for Life's role he's meant to play?
He ponders his destiny.

Then comes the Man from Galilee;
He's lifted up for all to see
upon the donkey small and gray,
led through streets of stone and clay.
He faces his destiny.

Crowds follow Him and wave green palms.
They shout hosannas, hymns and psalms.
For sins of ours this Man shall pay
This One, The Truth, The Life, The Way.
He has fulfilled his destiny.

A Christmas Prayer

Dear Baby Jesus, touch and bless
our loved ones near and far.
Light their lives with Christmas love,
Your bright and wondrous star.
We celebrate with joyful hearts
Your coming--for Your birth
has given promise,
    lasting hope,
        of peace upon this earth.

He Is Coming

When my mailbox overflows
with greetings of holiday cheer
and I pen my annual visit
on paper,
when I listen joyfully
to familiar carols,
gather those I love and precious memories
even closer to my heart,
I feel a special kind of peace
and I know
The Child is near.

Happy Birthday Jesus

Star candles twinkle, glow
atop snow-frosted-cake of an earth
that sings, proclaims, celebrates
the Christ Child's Birth-day.

Just For Fun

Everyone smiles in the
same language

They Dance at the Ball

Dancing with her Prince,
black-velvet-gowned Princess Night
flirts with starry eyes.

Their waltzing feet glide
with soft music filling
a celestial ballroom.

As Dawn pulls her away,
she loses one glass slipper;
the Prince searches, searches.

He finds his love, Day –
blue-ginghammed Cinderella;
the glass slipper fits.

They wait for darkness.
Again she is Princess Night;
they dance at the ball.

Mismatch

From large display, I choose a box
that holds one pair of nylon socks.
"Knee-hi's" it reads to my delight,
the color's great, the price is right.
The label reads, Size No. 9,
to stretch and fit feet large as mine.

I pay, go home, to my dismay,
one sock comes up just half the way.
I'll wear my slacks so it won't show
that they don't match, no one will know.
Won't take them back, I'll be a sport
and just pretend one leg is short.

A Strictly Legal Business

The sky is a giant still;
a bright, round-faced moonshiner
extends a bibulous invitation
to attend his night party.
He ladles a lunar liquid
with a starry dipper
from an immense black sky-kettle,
dispenses it generously.
I drink freely,
become intoxicated from the cascade
of bubbling, luminous spirits.

Daylight shuts the door
on this strictly legal business.
We wait for night to fall,
then the moon
again switches on its welcome light.
Join me for a walk,
come with me to the party,
imbibe with me in this refreshment.
Drink deeply,
enjoy the still exhilaration, the magic
of a heady autumn night.

The Gardener???

I shopped and bought some fresh seed,
now I was a real gardener indeed.
Planted, watered seed right,
sun drenched them with light,
but alas, every sprout was a weed.

Afternoon Exchange

(of Phyllis Galagher and Bernie Bibbs)
My Kev and I go visiting
friend Bernie down the street.
The weather's cold, I dress him warm
from head down to his feet.

My friend and I drink coffee, talk,
the children merrily play.
I watch the mantle clock because
we must not overstay.

When time to go, I bundle him
while perched upon my knee.
Bernie and I keep chattering,
Kevin tries to wriggle free.

I "shush" him up, keep dressing him,
Why does he seem so wild?
I turn him 'round to add his cap,
Good grief, it's not my child!   (It was Bernie's Jeff.)

Fall LOMP Seminar, Assisi Heights, Rochester, MN, October 1992.

Assisi Sights

On picturesque and peace-filled hill
we poets met; we always will
remember all the learning fun,
the friendliness of everyone.

My rest was comfortable, complete;
I dressed, unhurried, felt quite neat
until I realized with woe,
my skirt was backwards, "Oh my, no."

It made my skirt quite short in back,
too long in front, alas, alack.
But fashion mirrors Women's Rights,
I'll call new style "Assisi Heights."

94

Limericks

Marriage License

A fella named Kermit McDermott
chose to live life as a hermit.
    'Til one summer day
    a cute girl passed his way,
who brought along preacher and permit.

Where the Action Is

A beautiful princess named Alice
felt her life was quite dull in the palace.
    She said, "Life's too staid,"
    then decided to trade
her palace for condo in Dallas.

Fair Trade

I bought a neat gift for friend Garret.
It was Polly, a bright talking parrot.
    But of all the bad luck,
    a small cracker got stuck
in Pol's throat, so he tried to remove it.

He grabbed right ahold of this bird,
who sat there, not speaking a word.
    He started to whack her
    and out popped the cracker,
such cussing you never have heard.

Now parrots that swear are too risky.
This Polly's a little too frisky.
    So I set the bird loose,
    gave Garret a goose,
and threw in a jug of fine whiskey.

Bee Wary

A delightful young lady named Rosie
bent over to pick a bright posie.
> She was unaware
> that a bee lingered there
'til it lit and it bit Rosie's nosie.

Bubbles in the Brine

Joey loved Chloe, my daughter.
He pursued and he wooed when he caught her.
> They went for a swim,
> my Chloe dunked him.
Joey sank 'cuz he drank too much water.

Vitamin Efficiency

Marma sat on the nest that I'd made.
When no eggs, the young hen was dismayed.
> I said, "Could it be
> you need Vitamin C?"
Now in the nest rests the orange Marma laid.

Nutty Accommodations

A grower of pecans named Pete
took a trip to the Island of Crete.
> He checked in at an inn;
> the clerk said with a grin,
"Hows about the Nutcracker Suite?"

For Susan Chambers

Faster Than a Speeding Bullet

A young lawyer named Susan drove me
to Duluth, MN to share poetry.
　　Oh, we sped, I must tell
　　like a bat out of —well—
Susan drives like she writes, yesiree.

*My thanks to Sue, a national prize-winning poet and critic, daughter of
South Dakota poet, Barbara Stevens, mother of two young poets,
Christina and Colin. She is current president of the LOMP, future presi-
dent of the National Federation of State Poetry Societies. Sue is never
to busy to be a helpful sharing friend.*

Substitution

While on a vacation in Vail,
Dale looked for some good skis on sale.
　　But prices were high,
　　so he didn't buy,
just slid down the slopes in a pail.

Druthers

A young butcher named Terry Mahoney
gave his girl-friend a ring that was phony.
　　She complained, "It's a fake!
　　I 'd druther take
and wear a real ring of baloney.

The Question,
Which Craft?

There once was a mixed up old witch
who didn't know which way was which.
So she chartered a plane,
where she landed was Maine,
she'd parked her broomstick in the ditch.

This witch-tale takes on quite a switch.
A fisherman gave her a pitch.
She answered, "I'd 'otter'
stay clear of the water.
Guess I'm not sea, but a sand-witch."
The Answer,
Which Craft?
Not a plane or a boat, but her broom.

Good Intentions

I went up to the attic,
but I really must confess,
I took a sentimental journey,
left the attic still a mess.

Guilty As Charged

My son and his best friend named Davey,
enlisted as cooks in the Navy.
But while helping with mess,
they had to confess
to the crime of hard lumps in the gravy.

Practical Impracticality

1952   New hubby brought me holey sock,
        requested, "Honey, fix it."
        Since I hate to mend so much,
        I figgered I'd just nix it.

1966   A mound of mending waited long.
        My conscience prodded, "Do it!"
        I handed Mark his baseball suit,
        to find he had "out-grew" it.

1970   I spied Dave's jeans with missing knee.
        I'd promised to replace it.
        I cut 'em off for shorts instead.
        "This ain't my line, let's face it."

1976   Dan's favorite shirt was in the stack,
        kept hoping I would mend it.
        If only I had lots of cash,
        on new clothes I would spend it.

1981   I fought the mending battle, yes,
        and sometimes even win it.
        When Peter came with collar torn,
        I did not sew, I'd pin it.

1986   Today I heard the neatest quote,
        am planning to emboss it,
        and frame the sweetest words of all,
        "Don't mend the thing, just toss it!"

I guess I was a Mom, born a generation too soon.
Now it's fashionable to wear raggedy clothes.
Today, I could have sailed through life guilt-free!

Aqua Antics

The doctor says, "For achey bones,
move about in water,
keep muscles tight and body trim."
Guess we really "oughter".

With swimming suits and towels packed,
we head down to the Y's
heated pool to splash and swim
and water exercise.

We all wade in. WOW! This is fun,
but really, no surprise
that when our bodies are submerged
the water's sure to rise.

We stretch and reach and kick and hop
when Kathy calls out, "Yell!"
We jump as high as we can go
and holler just like – well – (loud).

We circle knees and rocking horse;
we alphabet-icize.
An exhilarating feeling is
our very special prize.

The lifeguard hauls the milk jugs out;
they are to help us float.
I stay down in the shallow end;
I need a raft or boat.

The camaraderie is great!
Golden Classics are a smash.
So keep a comin' to the "Y"
With smiles and jokes and splash!

New Growth

I had a little accident;
it was really quite "upsotting"
until I found that fall time
was a good time for repotting.

Jim had just retired and was hospitalized with pericarditis. On the way up to visit him at the hospital, I fell and broke my "write" wrist. I was carrying a little African violet which flew through the air when I fell. One morning, about six months later, after much therapy, our retirement plans on hold, I spied three buds on the violet and then I knew we were all going to make it. A year later I fell again and broke my shoulder. Dr. Markey, my orthopedic friend, suggested I write:

An Ode for a Klutz

Doc Markey said, "Oh no, not you,"
when I came in, arm black and blue.
"Oh yes, I took another trip.
On Sherman Street, my foot did slip
on patch of mud, I went kerplunk,
I swear to you, I wasn't drunk."

My hands flew up as down I went,
my bum hands grazed the cold cement.
Doc took X-rays, "Oh, holy smoke,
left shoulder shows a bone that's broke."
He hangs my arm into a sling,
clumsy bird with one clipped wing. (again)

This really ain't no ode, don't show it
to any bona-fide real poet.
For if you do, I'm sure I'll be
found hanging from a "Poet-Tree".

Another year later, another fall, a broken left wrist. No poem this time, just a prayer, "Slow me down, Lord and Keep me upright."

Growing Older

I used to be so young and agile
but now I'm getting old and fragile.
My eyes are getting so much dimmer
and yes, I'm plump, not getting slimmer.
My cane's my constant friend you know,
my hearing's going, gate is slow.
Safe former travels I recall
I'd like a TRIP without a fall.

It's only a verse; I'm really not in this bad shape!

Hold Up

I lean upon my trusty friend.
Sometimes my unsound knee won't bend.
But I go so fast I've often found
my tricky stick don't touch the ground –

Un-Caney.

*(At Fiesta Village in Mission, Texas, they laughingly, but kindly, refer to
me as the lady with the cane that can't keep up to her.)*

Perfect Partners

Seems I cannot live without you.
You have stuck through thick and thin.
Am I addressing hubby?
No, a trusty safety pin.

*(I kept losing my nametag at the North Mankato
Mud Lake reunion until I found a safety-pin
in my purse.)*

102

I was invited by Roberta Bartholdi, grandson Brian's third grade teacher, to share some poetry with the class. Lots of fun!

The Astro Cat

Elmer, sealed in his space suit
made of bright orange, glow-in-the-dark material,
is ready for count-down — 10-9-8-7-6-5-4-3-2-1
BLAST OFF!
The moon is orange tonight,
Elmer must have landed.
I wonder – when he returns,
will he leave moon-dust on my carpet?

Sky Santa

The winter sky is blue and bright.
I watch clouds drift with child's delight.
Amongst the clouds I see a face,
old Santa Claus in outer space.

His puffed cloud beard is soft and white,
I try to keep him in my sight.
But suddenly he's off, away,
the reindeer clouds pull large cloud sleigh.

She Fooled Me

My friend gave me a fuzzy pet.
It surely was the bunk.
I thought it was a pussy cat
but it really was a skunk.

Why Guess-T Towels?

Berry
Terry
Towels rest,
Handy
Dandy
Wait for guest.

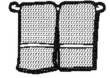

Tint, green
Hint, seen
Near my sink,
Bluish
Newish
Red, light pink.

Pick one
Thick one
I'm bemused,
Purely
Surely
Never used.

Biking Around Spring Lake Park

Cattails grow in crowds.
Marsh-people watch walkers, bikers,
pass in parade
season by season.

Vacation and Leisure

Sharing the beauty and excitement of our country with growing boys
was fun, educational, togetherness.
We tented, slept in a trailer or under the stars,
enjoyed campfires, s'mores, hot dogs.
We toured the Black Hills, Yellowstone,
Vancouver Island, Mackinac Island,
oohed and aahed the grandeur of Lake Louise.
We delighted in the sights and sounds of
our own great state of Minnesota: fished, swam,
stone stepped the beginnings of
the mighty Mississippi at Lake Itasca, circled Lake Superior, admired
the Boundary Waters.
It all happened in the long ago, but what precious memories.
Who says, "You can't take 'em with you?"

Colorado Collage

Summer, 1979

gondola ride view
slopes wait for sheer-white magic
to free ski spirits

Return trip, Winter 1980

see, we have returned
summer dreams now have come true
mountain snow greets us

boots, skis, poles, goggles
skiers, young, old, big and small
Jim and Pete join throng

ski spirits, now reality
Dad and Pete, slide, glide on
winter's white magic

Dan and I chatter
hot cocoa, cozy fireplace
(please, Lord, no broken bones)

time flies like snowflakes
lift closes, ski gear returned
a mountain of fun

hot springs soothe bone aches,
savory lake trout consumed
it's time to go home

Worship Service

Pine tree spires
rise above a campground cathedral,
its sanctuary filled with the music
of laughter,
motors whirring, birds singing.
Green leaves and fragrant wildflowers
adorn its altar.
A summer sun's rays touch
a shimmering lake,
remind us of the warmth and
brightness of God's love.
Campfires flicker, glow
like altar candles.
Incense– the smell of bacon frying,
coffee perking.
I feel His presence all around me
in our instant camping friends,
in meandering clouds,
the breeze
rustling aspen leaves,
in the hand that holds on to mine.
I bow my head.

Great Lakes' Fury

Tossed boats
Lost boats
Sailors fate,
Tearful
Fearful
Loved ones wait.

Gnashing
Smashing
Jaw-like waves,
Carry
Bury
In lake graves.

107

Florida

Variety Show

Sky theatre invites us all
to Sunday matinee.
We hear a famous Puppeteer
is on the bill today.

The stage hands pull cloud curtain back
and so, "On with the show."
Sky puppets pantomime on stage;
we watch, entranced, below.

Magician taps his wand. Behold,
cloud disappears, and then
He dips his hand into His hat
and brings cloud back again.

The animals, well-trained, perform;
their feats and tricks excite.
The dancers dance and acrobats
jump, tumble with delight.

The closing act has just begun,
cloud birds tip feathered wings.
I shut my eyes and visualize
THE MAN who pulls clouds' strings.

Emerald Coast Bonus

Sun rays sparkle Gulf,
mingle with blue-green water,
sugar sand — warm toes.

Winter Morning Contrast
((Material Witnesses)

Mankato, Minnesota, January 28, 1989

Crowd of crows create
black geometric design
on gray broadcloth sky.

Destin, Florida, February 3, 1989

Graceful airborne gulls'
off-white feathers pattern
blue velveteen sky.

Destin, Florida, February 10, 1989

Bolts of unrolled fog
hide sky. Gulf, white splashed
on emerald taffeta.

Mankato, Minnesota, March 30, 1989

Spring Marches, colors streak,
are caught, silk screened
on fabric of HOME.

Hand Out

Feathered beach beggars,
sea gulls swoop, dip, glide,
grab tossed food–
free meal ticket.

Leftovers

Tide washes away
life's sand castles.
Afterthoughts– sea shells
dot heart's shore.

Surfside Valentine

We leave behind the cold and snow,
head South for Gulf of Mexico.
We stroll its beaches hand in hand,
Jim traces heart in firm, white sand.

We gather shells and I am kissed,
by my love, Jim, Gulf wind and mist.
Sun caught in gleam of wedding band,
Jim traces heart in firm, white sand.

Our spirits touch, waves roll, meet shore
of Emerald Coast; gulls glide, land, soar.
Life, Earth and Sea, at God's command,
Jim traces heart in firm, white sand.

Holiday at the Beach

White sands are handy,
light hearts are dandy.
Sun brightened warm days,
fun heightened beach ways.
Strolling feet meet sand,
rolling waves greet land.

Lumpy dunes, sea oats,
bumpy waves, large boats.
See the sea soaring,
"Whee!" hear surf roaring.
Make Life a sensation,
take beach vacation.

Arizona

Snowbirds

Tourists,
we feign to be natives.
They smile, watch us try to blend.
They know that soon we must
go back to snow, so they let us
pretend.

To Reveal the Sun

The Silver bird ascends,
creates a vapor trail that chalk-lines
a blue slate sky.
Turbulent clouds splash rain
against glass panes,
Ever changing, they drift, disappear
to reveal the sun.

A downy comforter spreads
blanketing the sky;
cumulous clowns tumble with delight.
Beyond the window,
a bird image dips its wings
of feathered clouds
to reveal the sun.

Our silver carrier streaks toward earth.
I study the faces of people around me wondering
who they are, where they're going.
Wheels touch the ground.
Passengers scurry off like clouds,
disappear into an ever changing world
to reveal their sun.

Arizona Interlude

I'm captivated by this land
of sage and cactus, shifting sand,
where palm trees wave at passers-by
and mountains etch blue canvas sky.

The flowers, plants, fruit-heavy trees
and I respond to warm dry breeze
where coyotes roam, bold eagles fly
and mountains etch blue canvas sky.

My spirit sings as crystalled streams
and sun-splashed days surpass my dreams,
where God-brushed scenes delight the eye
and mountains etch blue canvas sky.

Southern Comfort

Each winter we become snow birds.
We soar away towards southern states
to bask in sun.

Chilled pair, from North to South,
we wing our way over mountain, desert roads
to bask in sun.

Leave shivers, shovels far behind,
we search to find our special place,
to bask in sun.

Each winter we become snow birds
to bask in sun.

Texas

TEXAS

(McAllen, Texas 1991)

Winter Tex-Suns

"Buenos Dias."
We Northerners, who move, migrate
from cold and snow to the Lone Star State,
in wintertime now celebrate
in the valley of the Rio Grande.

You share your wealth of sunlit days.
We cherish mem'ries, leisure ways,
and for it, Lord, we give You praise
in the Valley of the Rio Grande.

Historic, picturesque and fun,
it seems to grow on everyone.
We hope to leave our bit of sun
in the Valley of the Rio Grande.
"Adios Amigos."

Remember the Alamo

San Antonio, Texas

hushed
sight-see-ers
awed by the scene
visualize the old mission, turned fortress
besieged by Santa Anna and Mexican soldiers
blood shed
proud Americans lost their lives
we, too, are proud
to honor, praise, remember them.

113

Tearful Mission

Bus
plummets,
sand pit's
water
traps
school children —
four survivors.

Fence
holds names
flowers
pictures
I visualize faces
to match
the names.

We
return
each year
pausing
to remember
with saddened
hearts.

Our Lady of Guadalupe Parish

Attending Mass here is being "at home" with
friendly, family oriented people who
worship and mingle.
A dynamic priest, smiling Father Roy,
delivers his messages with punch.
His "Mama, Grandma" dog, Magna,
joins the priestly procession,
marches up the aisle,
lays down at the altar, wanders about,
A CELEBRITY,
the parish family's best friend,
faithful, church-going dog.

The Return

From the Northland's cold winters
to the Rio Grande Valley,
in a leisure and fun land,
Winter Texans, we rally.

Entertainment and culture,
sharing warm-weather pleasure,
friendly locals to greet us,
old and new friends to treasure.

Here there's golfing and dancing,
you can craft, shop with glee.
You can go Mexico-ing,
shelling, Gulfing is free.

You can fish, swim or shuffle;
fruits and veggies home-grown.
As we live here among you,
we feel completely at home.

Thanks for sharing your Valley;
it is really fulfilling.
We'll come back again next year
if the good Lord is willing.

(We've found our winter "place in the sun" at Fiesta Village in Mission, Texas)

115

A Mesquite Show of Spring

I look skywards, see the beginnings
of a new seasonal spectacular on the stage
of the Rio Grande Valley's sky theater.
The leading lady emerges from the wings.
With her feet on the ground,
her head in the clouds.
Senorita Springtime seems to dance.

She swirls and twirls her wavy green skirt
of maturing mesquite leaves.
Her blouse is of a delicate azure.
Bleached white tresses spill out
from beneath a lacy mantilla
that is pinned with a small cumulus hairbow,
ribboned with golden sunbeams.

Other stars join in this wind-choreographed production.
The stage is filled with growing excitement.
Awed by the beauty and graceful movements
of the cast, I gratefully whisper
my thanks to the Producer.

I snap mental photographs
to be developed later,
to take home to our North Country,
to remember this charming Southern Lady
and her entourage,
to capture and preserve
our treasured together time of sharing
of this pleasurable
SHOW OF TEXAS E-MOTION.

Friends
Neighbors
School
Community

In community we find hope
In hope we find dreams
With dreams we pull together...

From "Poetic Paraphrase..."

For dear neighbor and friend, Alice Perrizo Thomas

Second Sight

I have a very special friend
whose sight is now quite dim,
but Alice doesn't turn from God,
her eyes are set on Him.
She tells of many precious sights
reflected in her mind;
she sees so many things we miss;
we see, but yet are blind.

She sees a happy voice, a smile,
sound pictures in her ear.
She sees in the feel of a loved one's touch,
their joy in being near.
She sees with winter's icy blast,
bright springtime sun's warm rays;
sees summer in the smell of flowers,
leaves' crunch of autumn days.

Her fingers see her rosary beads,
each bead a call to pray.
She asks for God's and Mary's help
so many times a day.
She says a sense of humor helps,
cures may of life's ills,
that laughter works much better,
than a myriad of pills.

Sometimes I stop and close my eyes,
thank God with all my might,
with gratitude for eyes that see
and for an inner sight.
The lesson my friend Alice taught,
that seeing is an art,
her message, we must close our eyes
and learn to see with HEART!"

For American Legion Auxiliary friend, Beanie Wersal and her friend.

Chilled Chablis

This house in a strange new town
is quiet;
furniture and bits of nostalgia do not make it home.
Emptiness permeates
unfamiliar rooms, my spirit,
we are far away from yesterday.

I light the candle on the mantle,
part of your going away present.
A candle,
two goblets and a bottle of wine
remind me of our friendship.

I take a crystal wine glass,
fill it with
chilled chablis,
sparkling as your laughter.
The empty feeling disappears,
your warmth touches across the miles.

I pick up the phone, "Hello,
just called to say how much
I miss you.
No, we will never be far away,
close as a phone call, a letter,
a memory,
a candle, two goblets and a
bottle of wine."

For my wonderful friend, Elizabeth Congdon Pengel

The Sharing

My bike stops at the white colonial house,
a magnet of love pulls me up the steps.
Elizabeth greets me with smile and embrace.
We drink from flowered china cups–
tea, instant like our friendship.

Conversation flows
like water from a rainspout; we share
secrets, recipes, prayers, joys, hurts.
Ed passes through the kitchen,
manages to get in a few words
edgewise.
The clock chimes,
it's time to go home.
With another hug we thank God
for our precious gift of friendship--
tea, and tears,
tea, and laughter.

The Music Box

You are a cherished keepsake,golden, intricate, durable.
Your sparkle brightens
the corners of my heart,
your intrinsic beauty colors my days.
You paint a bouquet of lasting flowers
for me on the porcelain lid of life.
Your spirit lifts the cover
and I hear your music–
a song of faith, joy, compassion.
I sing along, love tunes
to remember and cherish.

Neighbors

You folks next door, across the street,
down the block,
all good neighbors
are a treasure.
When I've needed a cup of sugar, a ride,
a friend, someone to share a joy or sorrow,
you have always been there.

It is true:
"To have a good neighbor
you must also be one."
I hope we have filled the bill for you, too.

In a broader sense, we all must learn
to be neighbors to one another—
family, strangers, needy, aged, handicapped,
oppressed or lonely.

We learn to see others' needs,
share happy times and sad times,
appreciate, accept, reach out to one another.
For I believe:
"Neighborliness is next to Godliness."

People Craft

people
strands of hemp
macramae knotted together
become plant hangers
to hold flower pots of
friendships
we hang them in heart's window
to grow

So, Who Is Sue?

Write-ly, brightly, she meets life,
fine gal, mine pal, Willie's wife.
Choosey, Suzey, meals and tea,
hostess, mostest, Glenna Dee.
Sharing, caring, mother, friend,
giving, living, smiles – no end.
Sun-caught, fun-fraught, stays in sight,
she bakes, she makes life – DELIGHT.

(Sue is my old neighbor, Clara Moses' daughter-in-law.)

The Visit

I wili not let this trip
to the nursing home depress me.
Instead, I will smile and receive smiles
grasp an outstretched hand,
clasp a feeling of caring.

I will go home thanking God
for patience and dedication of
doctors, nurses, care-givers.
One day, much sooner than
I'd like to think,
I could be on the other side
of this visit.

Then, I hope there is a someone
to tend my needs, care,
smile, receive my smile
and hold my hand.

For Diane and Peter

Pals

Diane:

I hope someday when you're all grown up,
you'll look back to when you were three
and remember a carefree child's world
where your "bestest friend" was me.

When we rode your horse and scooted our trikes,
when we colored and played games galore,
when we played house and I was the Dad,
a grown-up man of four!

There were other kids to play with
and we enjoyed them, too.
But the mostest fun we had was when
there was only me and you!

May we always share this memory,
though we are miles apart.
Remember you were the very first girl
that stole a piece of my heart!

And when our grown-up world consists
of other guys and gals,
remember all the fun we had
when we were little pals.

Peter

Wheeler Park, First Day of School

The bare elm branches
move with hot September winds;
trunks painted with red D, wait.

Green grass begs for touch
of bare feet, now "shooed" beneath desks.
Summer is over.

Lonely playground toys
sit in quiet rejection;
where is the laughter?

Outdoor tables think
of plump hot dogs, lemonade,
families sharing.

Joy! Here come
the kids out for recess;
school's out at three.

Park and children
meet to share one another;
park's tears, now dried.

Holy Rosary School Tree Blessing

Earth,

accept this sapling,
let it take root.
Trees like children
need time and nurturing
to mature.

Lord,

warm them all with Your sunshine,
make them grow,
strengthen them with Your raindrops,
and the reign of Your LOVE.

For Cecelia Weaver (1899-1995)

The Weaver

You wove your talents
of education, music, poetry,
blended them with a bright constant faith
created a shawl of help and friendship.
Beneath your shawl
you pulled me close
and warmed my heart.

For my poet friend, Dr. Roy B. Moore (1908-1993)

ForeverMoore

Roy made us giggle, he made us laugh
he left his smile as autograph.
He played his tunes (harmonica) we sang along.
He made us feel that Life's a song.
He went away, yet he's still here,
he left us poems and memories, cheer.
An extra-special down-home guy,
he called me Sunshine,
but he was Sky.

Sister Odile - Ever An Ideal

When I was in fourth grade,
Sister Odile and I formed an ever-lasting friendship.
A Fransican nun,
teacher, catechist, social worker,
she is a model of Christian womanhood.

For my wonderful teachers, my excellent teacher-aunts, and all good teachers.

Design for Living

You have woven your spirited pattern
    into the texture
      of my life.
Sunny threads of education, firmly stitched,
    blend with enduring strands of
      growth and friendship.

You helped me fashion a garment
    for living, sewed your seams of learning
      with discipline and dedication.
You added your own trimmings:
    the rickrack of responsibility,
      the lace of love,
then fastened securely
    your knot of knowledge.

Why is it,
    I am older,
      but you are ageless?

Perhaps, it is because all good teachers
    keep mind and heart so busy
      that there is no time to get old.
Now, still strong, golden threads remain,
    remind us of the days
      when we grew together.
Part of your early, unique design
    is still evident in the fabric of my life,
      worn with pride and thankfulness.

(Good Counsel Academy, Mankato, Minnesota, my alma mater)

Senior Homeroom Business

Sister Mary Alphonse smiles from heaven,
always with us in spirit.
We affectionately return her smile
in remembrance.

For Sister Honora , my high school English teacher, my friend

Art Instructor

Teacher,
dedicated, patient,
understanding.
She showed us how to diagram a sentence,
bake a cake, hem a dress,
but most of all,
by her generous giving,
taught the greatest art
is sharing one's heart.

For Sister Kathryn

Row, Row, Row Your Boat

She rows her boat
with a trusty pen for an oar,
looks for direction from
the Divine Navigator.

*In loving memory of Msgr. Alton H. Scheid, Chaplain, Good Counsel
Academy for 37 years, mentor, friend, now my special saint. I asked
Sister Kathryn to read this to Father shortly before he went to Heaven.*

February 1994

You wait patiently
for Heaven's grand reunion.
Cherished, prized friend,
you are LOVE
forever and ever.

March 24, 1994

I am informed of your death.
Though miles apart
and separated from you
by your eternity,
you are with me.
I hear heavenly GCA
cheerleaders
call out
"Rah, rah, rah,
A-L-T-O-N H. S-C-H-E-I-D!"

Sister Mary Ellen Rhys

October 1982
Brilliant, but humble instructor,
teaches of parallelograms,
God and sonnets, square roots, war
and literature.
She paints with water-colors,
oils and Memos of GCA.
Her eyes twinkle as she hides
a smile behind a big, white hanky.

With thanks to Sister Elizabeth Johannes, SSND, former Alumnae Director, editor of ReEchoes and all who have followed in her steps, as well as all GCA teachers, classmates, and alumnae.

Golden Gathering, Class of 1944

Reunion, Good Counsel Academy, Mankato, Minnesota, April 30, 1994

So many years, can you believe,
since we shared our Yesterday,
when we graduated, said, "Good-bye"
at dear old GCA?

We stop, recall the sights, the sounds
the sisters, Father Scheid
and Our Lady of Good Counsel
a Mother, ever at our side.

Our clocks turned back to yesterday,
we embrace, share teen-y laughs,
then seal this happy gathering
with prayers and photographs.

Homecoming

Fifty years have passed.
Now matured teens
relive school days.
Yesterday ReEchoed.

Once again
Our Lady of Good Counsel
holds us close
to Jesus, to herself,
tenderly.

For Father Ed Ardolf, pastor at Holy Rosary Parish, North Mankato, Minnesota

Father Ed

I know a very special man,
his name is Father Ed.
He's there for every one of us,
this keeps him in good stead.
He preaches and he teaches us
with stories – quite a few.
He never seems to "runneth out"
of jokes both old and new.

He's full of life and lives it well.
His heart is filled with song
of children, faith and family,
we join his sing-along.
He is a happy, generous man,
his big smile cheers the heart.
He glues us back together, when
we seem to fall apart.

He is the shepherd of the flock
at Holy Rosary.
He pulls us all together with
Sociability.
He visits sick and elderly;
we know he really cares.
He keeps us on our toes and knees;
he lives his daily prayers.

He wears a jaunty little cap;
and energy—no end!
He wears his priesthood with great pride—
our pastor, neighbor, friend.

For the mothers of our priest friends, Fathers Adrian Piatrowski,
Jim Motl, Tim Hodapp, and Doug Grams.

These Hands

I see two dimpled infant hands
that hold a small stuffed toy.
These precious little hands belong
to your dear baby boy.
A pair of busy toddler hands
play with a truck or car;
I see them stealing cookies, too,
out of your cookie jar.

I see two hands all full of dirt,
they offer you mud pies.
They pull a wagon, steer a trike,
I see two sparkling eyes.
These hands shoot marbles, catch a ball,
or swing a baseball bat.
They mow the lawn and help their Dad,
stop to pet a dog or cat.

A communicant or altar boy,
hands folded tight in prayer,
diploma in his teenaged hands,
recollections that you share.
Years have a way of moving on,
these boyish hands have grown.
Hands of a priest belong to God,
Christ chooses them, His own.

"Dear God," we ask,
"please bless these hands,"
this fervent prayer we pray,
"that they may serve You long and well,
and honor You each day."

To Father Charles Kerr, S.J., Sts. Peter and Paul Parish, Mankato.

Priest

first, last and always.
Cherished friend, photographer par excellente,
armed and ever-ready to "shoot" anyone in sight
with your trusty camera,
you make kids, young and old
laugh as you clown and "tweet-tweet".
Generous with your time and talent,
you peddle prints, reprints
and sunshine,
capture wonderful moments
for un-countable folks.
One fantastic guy!

For Father Terry Brennan, S.J., Sts. Peter and Paul Parish priest.

Our Very Own Irish Blessing

I know a young priest, wise and merry,
a Brennan, his name, Father Terry.
He has charm, songs and smile—
shades of "The Emerald Isle"—
and loving, of course, he is VERY!

His vocation is deep and sincere,
serves his Lord with a heart full of cheer.
He greets with a letter
and nobody's better
at revealing his feelings, he's dear.

We are blest in a friendship so rare,
entrusted to Jesus with care.
Though we're now far apart,
he is ever in heart
and we're bonded for always in prayer.

132

For Isabelle Neitge Johnson, North Mankato librarian and friend.

Librarian

I hope someday that I will see
my vibrant friend once more.
That will be a special blessing
that Heaven holds in store.
There she will be, among the books,
as busy as can be.
I will ask if she will take her stamp,
check out THE BOOK for me.

*For Bill Johnson, Isabelle's husband, our neighbor, who showed us
what faith and determination can accomplish.*

The Perfect Healing

The ramp
that led up to the big brick house on Sherman Street
disappeared.
I can see Bill climb Heaven's steps;
Strong limbs carry him
Home.

When Heaven Calls

No, Not Good-bye

Auf Wiedersehen	German
Au Revoir	French
Vaya Con Dios	Spanish
Arrivederce	Italian
Slan Leat	Irish
Lykke pa reisen	Norwegian

'Til we meet,
'Til we greet again,
We will remember.

In loving memory of Chris and Marne, 1979

Star Light

I walk tonight in crisp, cool air
with signs of autumn everywhere.
The leaves drift down and stars light night;
with awe, I feel God's power, might.
Oh, twinkle, twinkle, little star,
I wonder who, or what you are.

Then suddenly it comes to me—
perhaps it is, you're meant to be
hung there in place, a sparkling gem
to glow in Kingly diadem
in memory of someone held dear,
though gone away, yet always near.

For Gert Kelly (1900-1995) my priceless neighbor, friend, a 74 year
charter member of CDA and for all CDA's.

Catholic Daughters of the Americas

Court St. Rose of Lima 60th Anniversary, October 1980

We Daughters wear a diamond brooch,
each one of us a lustrous stone,
glowing like candles on our birthday cake.

The facets of each stone have been cut,
polished with acts of charity.
A Divine Jeweler sets each gem in its place,
creates a dazzling pin.

We wear it proudly, as members of CDA.
Called to spread God's Love
to others, we help make the Americas
and the whole world a better place to live.

Chicken Club

It seems almost everybody
has heard about our famous group.
Now eighteen members, we gals
meet monthly, share our faith-filled
FRIENDSHIP,
laughter and prayers, concerns and joys,
and a chickeny meal.
We thank God for this little flock;
it is really something
to crow about.

Chatter, Chatter, Cluck, Cluck

Colonel Sanders cooks the chicken.
Hens dine, cluck with caring hearts,
Interesting, inclusive
Chatter, chatter.
Kentucky Fried's cook lets hostess visit.
Each in turn sets a festive table, serves dessert.
Nifty ladies, never gossipy, share news.

Camaraderie, closeness, comfortableness,
Love of God, one another, fill us with
Understanding and unity. Like the Colonel's
Buttered biscuits, warm and honey-spread,
    our hearts enjoy and savor this taste of togetherness.

Wait--Loss

You nibble veggies crisp and cool;
you say, "No, no," to sweets — the rule.
And when you find cholesterol high,
you grab a peach instead of pie.

If you would like to drop some weight,
to feel that you are lookin' great,
to gaze in mirror with "figger" svelte
or put another notch in belt,

you nibble veggies crisp and cool
and say, "No, no," to sweets — the RULE!

(With a well rounded figure, I have found refusing goodies to be lots easier said than done. While I was on a diet, I was watching ducks at Spring Lake Park, when I penned the following verse.)

Quick-Quack Verse

A round, fat duck stood open mouthed,
begging for goodies and bread.
A skinny duck quacked to the lake
and took a swim instead.

The moral is: if round and fat,
don't tempt yourself with caloried snack.
Just waddle off to excercise,
use your mouth to quack, quack, quack.

Gratitude

Dear God,

Tomorrow, when day breaks, I'll be
a life that's spanned a century.
I turn back now to childhood dreams,
to happy, carefree times. It seems
like yesterday I walked the aisle,
took husband's hand, looked up to smile.

Our home, secure, a happy place,
You shared with us, blessed with Your grace.
Life held its problems, burdens, cares,
You smoothed them over, answered prayers.
You gave us children, lively, sweet,
they kept us young, made life complete.

A cake to bake, a dress to sew,
a garden plot to plant and hoe.
Our family and friends the height
of joy; when grandkids came—delight.
Ten decades lived, Your gift of days
for 36,525, I give You praise.

Can You believe, one hundred years
of laughing laughs and crying tears?
Of course You know, for it was You
who gave me life, made dreams come true.
You walked with me, You showed me how
to live and love, You've granted now
a celebration of my 100th birthday.

137

For Sal Frederick after his last legislative term
as a Minnesota State Representative.

A Winner

The election's over, the votes are in.
The trouble is, just one can win.
You'll take this loss, right in your stride
new heights to reach, Rose at your side.

We thank you for your dedication.
You've served us with deliberation.
So take your bows, the records tell
you were effective, worked pell-mell.

For Ken Berg, Holy Rosary classmate (1937-40), on his
retirement as Mankato Free Press Editor.

Pen Pusher

A newspaper editor, Ken
earned his livelihood pushing a pen.
With printer's ink in his blood
covered life, fire and flood.
I remember he wrote way back when.

Kenny, my good friend, has heart,
but sometimes could blow us apart
when the pages of press
would cause us distress,
make feelings tingle and smart.
(*A periodical needs a little controversy, I guess*)
A newsy career is exciting,
but leisure and fun are enticing.
My retirement rhyme:
"Have a heckuva time,
but remember, Ken,
always keep writing."

Remember When

It seems there was a treat in store,
North Kato kids could meet once more
in Spring Lake Park to reminisce,
"A good idea, who thought of this?"

Jim Lynard thought it would be neat,
if some of their old gang could meet.
The Mud Lake bunch would come and then
they'd play the game REMEMBER WHEN.

The idea mushroomed, grew and grew,
how many'd come, nobody knew.
We came from town, from far and near,
a single purpose brought us here.

We shared our memories, photographs,
we turned back time, had lots of laughs.
How blest we are, how much we care,
with heritage so strong and rare.

And those who came to celebrate
found fellowship and spirit great.
Oh yes, we all were HOME again
that day we played REMEMBER WHEN.

July 1992

Belgrade Avenue Improvements

June 1986

The dozers dig, my house doth shake,
now I know what they mean by quake.
Yards full of stakes, surveyors mark,
the thick dust flies, from dawn 'til dark.
The scoopers scoop, dirt, roots, and rocks,
the bob-cats bob, midst concrete blocks.
The dirt piles high, the holes, deep down,
I've learned "what's up" beneath our town.

Fork lifts and trucks blow whistles shrill,
I wish we'd bought up on the hill.
My fuse is short, my nerves are taut,
serenity cannot be bought.
The filled up holes make spirits soar
until they come and dig some more
to dash my hopes with such disdain.
Besides, they broke the water main.

Detours abound, blocked traffic lanes,
we moan and groan with growing pains.
New sewers too, "Oh, glory be!
I sure am glad they saved our tree."
Tanned worker teams seem quite adept;
concrete is poured, it's smoothed and swept.
The prayer I say, as this I view,
"Thank heavens for— curbs, gutters new."

The graders grade, the gravel spread,
"Next comes the tar," a worker said.
A brand new sidewalk soon in place
will put a smile upon my face.
Not patiently, I must confess,
I've waited out this awful mess.

August, 1986

Today they laid the sod and "Whee,"
the best improvement here is ME!!!

Poetic Paraphrase on Our Town, North Mankato

IF I were one of the old time masters of prose or poetry, a writer of yesterday's classics, or a well known author of today, perhaps I would express my feelings this way about *Our Town* – Thornton Wilder – " *Well, I'd better show you how our town lies. Right here is Main Street* (Belgrade Avenue), Mankato *proper is across the tracks.*"

"*How much do I love you, let me count the ways...*" -- Elizabeth Barret
    Browning.
    1. Lots of friendly people
    2. Parks and recreation
    3. Thriving businesses
    4. Well kept homes and property
    5. Police, fire protection
    6. Competent local government
    7. Churches, schools.

 "*I know I have the best of time and space...*" -- Walt Whitman.
    "Ditto, Walt."

A *Short Check List Of Things To Think About Before Being Born* -- John
    Ciardi--
    1. Choose the right parents
    2. Pick out the right town to be born in (North Mankato!)

"*My books and I are good friends...*" -- Edgar Guest.
    We have fine schools, library.

"*I think that I shall never see, a poem lovely as a tree...*" -- Joyce Kilmer.
    New trees, ash, maples, etc. replace ravaged elms; they too,
    "*lift their leafy arms to pray.*"

Midsummer Night's Dream -- William Shakespeare.
    No mosquitoes! "Right on, mosquito patrol!"

"*O my love is like a red, red rose...*" -- Robert Burnes.
    And like daisies, daffodils, grass.

I Stood Upon A High Place -- Stephen Crane.
    Lookout Point: where our eyes may glance downwards, span our
    "Twin Cities," look upwards to the part of the city that has climbed
    the hill.

"Dew drags a child over grass, a bird tastes a twig..." -- Michael Dennis
    Browne .
    And ducks beg for an early morning handout at Spring Lake.

Stopping By Woods On A Snowy Evening -- Robert Frost.
    Winter hikes on hillside trails.

The Bridge -- Hart Crane.
    We watch progress on the new bridge, joining us to over-town.

"And pleasant water courses, you could tract them through the valley..."
    Henry Wadsworth Longfellow .
    City nestled along and a-top the bluffs where the Minnesota and
    Blue Earth Rivers meet.

"I Am A Little Church, (no Great Cathedral) -- E.E. Cummings.
    Seven churches gather for worship to thank God for our blessings.

"How would you like to go up on a swing?" -- Robert Louis Stevenson.
    Or one can skate or swim, slide, play tennis; we've got parks, fun
    places, for old and young.

I Should Not Like To Leave My Friends -- Emily Dickenson.
    No one will ever entice me to leave North Mankato. Family,
    friends, we are joy to each other.

I Am The People, The Mob, The Crowd, The Mass -- Carl Sandburg.
    In community we find hope;
    in hope we share dreams,
    with dreams we pull together.
    Valley, hill, we blend,
    North Mankato, Minnesota ----
    proud city, people ----
    past, present, future!

The Inevitable

Dust, oh, we fight it constantly.
Unwise we fret and fuss.
Stop battle now, spend time with me—
Too late when dust is us!

When I leave there's sure to be

some dishes waiting in the sink,
some dust upon the sill,
some poems that need a final touch,
some promises, "I will..."

I never seem to finish up
all the projects that I start
for I must stop and share with you
some matters of the heart.

Perhaps

I haven't penned a poem for you
or mentioned you by name,
but know that I thank God for you;
you're remembered just the same.
And though the words aren't written down,
I've hoped I could impart
the fact that you're a precious poem
written on my heart.

Some of the publications in which Monica's writings have been honored to appear:

The Moccasin (*League of Minnesota Poets' publication*)
Heartsong and Northstar Gold (*LOMP Anthology, 1984*)
Poems of Praise
The Mankato Free Press
The Fulda Free Press
The LeCenter Leader
Heartbeat (*National Pro-life Magazine*)
New Ulm Diocesan Newsletter
Share (*Catholic Daughters of the Americas publication*)
Gopher News *(State Catholic Daughters Newsletter)*
ReEchoes *(Good Counsel Academy Alumnae newsletter)*
Full Circle Anthology (Editions 8, 9, 10, 11, 12)
Cottonwood Citizen (*Windom Newspaper*)
Living Waters (*River of Life newsletter*)
Midwest Chaparral Poets
The Advocate *(Minnesota Education Association publication)*
The Turning Wheel *(Southern Minnesota Poets' Anthology*
Mankato 30-40 Club Newsletter
The Mankato Shoppers' Guide
Church Bulletins
Holy Rosary Parish Cook Book
Fiesta Village, Mission Texas, Memorial Service
Immanual-St. Joseph Hospital Hospice 10th Anniversary
Winter Texan Senior News

In 1988 Monica received a citation from the city of North Mankato signed by Mayor David Dehen for her "Poetic Paraphrase of Our Town."

In 1991 Monica was included in an honoring of Minnesota poets at a Christmas reading at the State Capitol in St. Paul and was given a commendation by Governor Rudy Perpich.